MY PALESTINIAN AMERICAN LIFE

MY
PALESTINIAN AMERICAN
LIFE

Patricia J. Mousa

My Palestinian American Life

Additional copies may be ordered from the publisher for educational, business, promotional or premium use.
For information, contact ALIVE Book Publishing at:
alivebookpublishing.com, or call (925) 837-7303.

Book Design by Alex Johnson

ISBN 13
978-1-63132-267-9

Library of Congress Control Number: 2025924554

First Edition

Published in the United States of America by ALIVE Book Publishing
an imprint of Advanced Publishing LLC
3200 A Danville Blvd., Suite 204, Alamo, California 94507
alivebookpublishing.com

PRINTED IN THE UNITED STATES OF AMERICA

10 9 8 7 6 5 4 3 2 1

To the beautiful lives that have been lost in Palestine.

I did not know you, but I will never forget you.

And to my family, the ones that came before,
the ones here with me now,
and to those that come after,
you have filled me up.

"If the house of the world is dark, love will find a way to make windows."

-Rumi

"If you were born with the weakness to fall, you were born with the strength to rise."

-Rupi Kaur

Introduction

I have been thinking about my stories and the stories of so many other first generation Palestinians Americans.

Although many of their parents lost their homes and so much when they left, they proudly carried their culture and traditions with them to America, and these indelible things found their way into the hearts and minds of their children and the people they met in the new world.

For the endless and ongoing number of Palestinians that were forced to flee through history; although far from their homeland, some had families in the new places they traveled to.

Their families thrived; their families grew, and the Palestinian people expanded globally.

To all of us that came before and to those that came after, we are here, we are strong, and we will persevere.

Growing up in America as a daughter of Palestinian parents was at times filled with confusing and turbulent moments, but the pursuit of freedom and the promise of a better life that my parents must have hoped for translated into a mostly joy-filled life with each day bringing something new to appreciate.

Here I share some of my stories that speak with simplicity and love and tell of growing up as first generation in a complex environment.

My parents had five daughters, and as young girls, we had everything we could ever hope for, and yet, for me, there were always traces of grief in the air for what was left behind. I am witness to both the grief and the joy and to the boundless love and expectations my parents had for themselves and for us.

And so, I write of my life and hope to share a rich story filled with some embroidered details and colors of my heritage.

My parents lived their young lives in a Palestine that I will never see. What they saw and experienced there became the foundation that they built their new Palestinian American lives on. The love they have for their homeland spirits forward all the good and the gratitude I feel every day for the treasures they brought with them.

Contents

Dedication.......5
Introduction.......7
Daddy.......13
Jungleland.......21
Tata.......27
Stories.......35
Work.......43
Mom.......57
Friend.......73
Drive.......81
Vacations.......89
Weekends.......99
Neighborhoods.......107
Morning.......123
Food.......131
Change.......147
Parents.......159
Marriage.......167
Loved.......179
Children.......187
Music.......195
Questions.......207

Adventures....215
Art....221
Rise....227
Mentor....233
Rooms....241
Escrow....251
Hawaii....259
Outsider....265
Travel....271
Motherhood....281
Grandparents....289
Tradition....297
Mezzeh....305
Simplicity....311
Appreciation....317

DADDY

Daddy

My father was a remarkable person. When I say remarkable, I mean unlike any other. He had a grand curiosity and an immense sense of wonder. He was always figuring things out. I have so many memories of him reading, fixing things, watching animal shows on the TV, listening to talk radio, growing things, and cooking. All the things he did with great gusto. Growing up with my father was like being on an unending carousel of things to do.

I was one of five girls, but I saw myself as my dad's shadow. I followed him around as much as he allowed. I thought his day-to-day activities were fun, insightful, and usually very messy, all of which appealed to my curious nature.

I learned so much from him because he was always finding some way to keep his hands busy. Our family owned a grocery store (*mahal*), which was quite typical for Palestinian families coming to America. As you are reading this, I am guessing that at some point in your life, you have found yourself in one of the many Arab owned little grocery stores or delis that populate so many corners of America. When our dad was at our grocery store, I went along whenever I could. The ever-changing landscape of his day was fascinating to me. Whether I was watching him make sale signs by hand, listening to his friendly chats with customers, or smoking at the liquor counter, hanging out with him was always interesting. A worthy example of what might excite a child is when I would watch his lit cigarette that he mostly left on the edge of the counter, literally hanging over the edge with an inch-long ash about to drop. Those old wood counters had burn marks from his cigarettes along most of the edges. He did not do this at home, of course, well, not very often anyway.

I found it interesting years later how much he seemed to enjoy the lighting of the cigarette and not really the smoking of it. I wonder how many hundreds of dollars literally went up in smoke. Better in the air than in his lungs. So far, we innocent bystanders have remained unscathed by the secondhand smoke.

When I went to hang out or work with dad, he would let me do things that I may have been too young for, but I didn't mind. In fact, I loved it.

He would let me be at the register, and he would let me put the stock away. My oldest sister, Noel, and I would be all over the store doing whatever dad asked us to do. We had so much fun in those aisles and in the back room setting things up.

My favorite thing of all was when daddy let me help him with the butchering and setting up the meat case. He was mostly a self-taught butcher, and he was so good at it. The case was filled with beautiful cuts of meat and special local favorites like City Chicken, which was ground chicken, pork, and seasonings smashed all together and shaped around a short skewer to look like a chicken leg. Even as a young girl, daddy would let me make the City Chicken with him from time to time.

One highlight was during hunting season, when customers would bring in their freshly killed deer, and I would sit on a milk crate and watch my dad break the animal down and package it for the customer. I can still remember that terrible feral smell and hear the sound of him pulling down the hide. It was more exciting to me than it was frightening, especially as he would tell stories while he worked.

In those days, the early 60s, my dad cut all his own meat from the whole or half animal. He aged the meat right there, too. A young girl can learn so much about being resourceful in this productive environment. My father wasted nothing, and at an early age, I found this to be my favorite lesson.

My dad loved to gamble, and in my mind, his love for wasting nothing collided with his love for gambling. If you have ever lost money gambling, I imagine you can see the irony. My dad's love for gambling created tension at home. My dad was not perfect. He was neither concerned about that nor was he apologetic. He took things in stride and just did whatever he liked.

When he was not at the store or the racetrack, he was home with us playing in the park. Edward Hines Park was behind our house on Terri Drive in Westland, Michigan. We could go through the back gate and down to the park, which we did as often as mom or dad allowed. My dad loved to take us to the park, and we were always ready to go. During almost every trip to the park, at some point, you could find my dad lying down under a tree with his head propped up by an arm behind his head, taking a little nap. This image always made me smile, because for me it embodied the sense that all was well in the world.

I fell in love with nature through these numerous visits to the park and my dad's fascination with all things natural. He would point out birds, insects, leaves, and clouds. The Nankin Mills Nature Center was in that park, and he took us there dozens of times while we lived on Terri Drive.

He could do all manner of things; maybe not perfectly, but with loads of passion. He was not afraid to try his hand at anything. He was self-taught and enjoyed learning as he went along.

I imagine that he saw his immigration to America from his beloved Ramallah, Palestine, as the greatest leap of his life. He really did not have much choice as the Nakba of 1948 forced so many to flee in search of a better life. Their freedom and way of life was stolen. I have often wondered, does it take a remarkable person to leave their homeland in search of a better life, or does leaving your home and family make you remarkable?

A most remarkable person.

Shawky Jamil Mousa arrived in America in 1949

Daddy & Me

JUNGLELAND

JUNGLELAND

Children usually have memories of their favorite toys from when they were young. I have been thinking about this and scouring my memory to try and conjure up images of some favorite toys, or at least a single favorite toy. Unable to come up with anything, I am reminded of rummaging through old boxes and musty attics and not finding what you went there looking for.

Alas, I cannot recall any favorite toys from my childhood, except for maybe the marbles. Funny thing is, when I think about playtime as a child, the first thing that comes to mind is the park and the vast Michigan outdoors. I loved to play outside in nature. I guess you could say that my favorite things to play with were leaves, flowers, pollywogs, clouds, and trees. Being outside was so much fun, the biggest playground of all. We would gather pollywogs at the creek and put them in a jar and watch them turn into little frogs. I would watch the clouds, fabricate animals, and imagine all sorts of things within the clouds. There is nothing quite like those beautiful, engaging, and voluminous Michigan clouds.

I liked to crisscross twigs and build things with them, using leaves and grass to reinforce my structure. Trees were for climbing, of course, and for watching closely to see how they changed through the seasons. The same went for flowers. One could imagine all the different and magical places in the spaces that existed outside.

The most magical place was what we called Jungleland in the park directly behind our home on Terri Drive. I'm not certain of the origin of the name, but somewhere in growing up on Terri Drive, Jungleland, it became. I loved Jungleland so much that I would dream of its soft and safe spaces. In the spring, a beautiful bed of purple violets would emerge, and I used to love lying there and looking up at the tree canopy. I remember the flowers; so fragrant and tender, sharing the deepest violet color with anyone who walked through Jungleland and stopped to notice. I would go there each year to welcome their delightful entrance to my world. Jungleland was such a magical place to lie and wonder, a quiet place to escape to when mom was in a poor mood or when the chaos of home overwhelmed me.

Other outdoor activities with my sisters included running through the sprinkler, riding our bikes, and splashing around in our little pools. And best of all was when dad would come home from the store, and we would all go through our backyard gate and down to the park.

Our beloved park was filled with beautiful trees. I especially loved the wild sumac trees with their burnt red cascade of flowers. Sumac is a robust and tangy Palestinian spice that I use often, but I never made that connection as a child.

I loved wall ball on our backyard brick wall and basketball next door. The Fehlners lived next door, and over time, we got to know them pretty well. At times, in those first months, I could feel the sting of tension or a slight awkwardness that surrounded this gathering of cultures. They were white and we were not. It's amazing how the collection of the playing children settled those tensions. As an adult, I wondered if they really existed at all. Sometimes the feelings we remember are deep and intense and might be ours alone. I did notice and found it a little odd that we were allowed to play at their home and mostly in the backyard, but they rarely came to ours.

In our young lives, there was a second "Jungleland" which was our incredible basement. It was quite huge with lots of room to wander inside when the weather was bad. Mostly, this basement would get filled with the youngest members of our growing Palestinian American family. As the years went by, my father would sponsor many of our relatives, such as his siblings, and also his mother's passage to America. From time to time, various family members stayed with us until they were able to establish a home for themselves.

In our home, with the five girls and usually some cousins, we had a full crew of playmates at all times. We had many games to play in the basement, and I enjoyed playing with my sisters and learned to be competitive at an early age. I loved board games, shooting marbles, Parcheesi, checkers, hangman, tic-tac-toe, and pick-up sticks.

There in that basement, we would play hide and seek and tag. We had Lincoln Logs and lots of random mismatched blocks that allowed for a whole other level of imagined spaces and buildings for those of us who liked to build. Coloring was another favorite pastime and usually not in a coloring book but more freestyle on paper, where we would draw random swirls of interlocking lines and then fill the spaces with a beautiful arrangement of colors. I believe this single pastime (more of a compulsion) helped to wire my brain to visualize color and special balance in an aesthetic that worked for me. I loved to color like that and recently saw the same coloring at my children's home. Of course, I colored that way with my children and now my grandchildren.

If I liked dolls and things like that, I certainly do not remember them. I still don't care for dressing up much, and hairstyling and the like.

Playtime was about the engagement of sisters, cousins, and the contest of whichever game or project was at hand. A healthy competitive streak lives in me, and I recognized this early.

I mustn't forget the magic of my marbles. I liked to think that they were mine, but we shared all the toys, and that meant the marbles too. We had so much fun playing with marbles and coveting the best ones. I still have a big bowl of marbles, and I am fairly certain they are our childhood marbles because I remember carrying a bag of them from move to move. At least some of them, especially that beautiful pale green swirly one.

In the end it seems marbles are my favorite toy. I found them so sensory in every way; to hold between my fingers and roll around in my hand, to shoot them and then listen for the unique sound each one would make upon contact, and especially to hold each up to the sun and look through the myriad of colored and layered glass.

TATA

Tata

It wasn't until I was about nine or ten that I became aware of the fact that I was missing three grandparents in my life.

I had heard a few stories, but that was the extent of my awareness of them. I didn't fully yet comprehend that some children grow up with all their grandparents, or none of their grandparents, or somewhere in between. I had heard a few stories about my dad's father and my mom's parents, but sadly nothing so substantial that I could speak to them fully.

When I close my eyes and think about these lost three in my life, one story that stands out is about my maternal grandmother, *(Tata)* Azizeh Dirbas. She never saw her daughter Jannette again after she and my eldest sister Noel left Ramallah, Palestine and headed for Detroit to be with my Dad.

It is sad to think of the millions who left their native land, never to set eyes on family again. In those days, there were no apps or social media or even the certainty of a phone call. I feel lucky and blessed for so much privilege and access in my lifetime to interact with family that is far away.

The other grandparent story that left its mark is about my paternal grandfather, *(Sido)*Jamil Mousa, who sacrificed his lungs to mustard gas in a war that was not his. I wish I had asked my dad more stories about his father, but when I did, I could see pain in his eyes when he spoke of him.

Around age three, my dad's mom, Tata Zarifeh Mousa, came to America. My father bought her a ticket and made plans for her to immigrate to America. He subsequently did the same for his siblings and others, too.

Our tribe loved to gather with as much family as possible. This included aunts, uncles, and so many cousins, and some of their tatas and sidos too. We would visit for long periods of time to eat, visit, and tell stories. It was at those gatherings that the seeds of my future were planted. Those seeds were nurtured with every get-together and over the years, they grew into a stand of mighty trees that serve as the foundation of my existence.

As the migration from Palestine to Detroit grew, so did the number of cousins who came and lived close by. My youngest years are filled with memories of the parties to celebrate the arrival of each new member of our extended family.

When our Tata Zarifeh arrived from Ramallah, I am certain there was a big party (*Hafleh*) with much food and fanfare. Tata Zarifeh was a tough woman and one who demanded a certain respect along with an abundance of attention and adoration. As I grew older and especially during the times she stayed with us, I came to recognize this more and more. She loved to praise the grandchildren and the daughters-in-law who followed her wishes and behaved in the way she expected and deemed appropriate. She had four sons and five daughters.

As a granddaughter, I was always on the winning side, for my nature was domestic and I was fond of elders and of the kitchen and everything that took place there. Tata Zarifeh truly delighted in my passion for helping in the kitchen. I was also ready to serve and wait on the aunts and uncles, as was our custom. I have often wondered just how much of this constant praise for what the older generation thought was appropriate for young girls impacted my life and even my career.

One of my favorite stories that dad loved to tell about his mom, our wonderful Tata Zarifeh, had to do with the drive home from the airport on the day she arrived in America. On the leisurely drive home, dad was doing a little sightseeing and showing Tata some of the then-fancy Detroit boulevards. Tata was looking at the massive green lawns in front of the old prestigious homes as he was driving slowly by. She asked what they were growing in front of their houses. My father said, (in Arabic), "Those are lawns, it's grass." And her response was, "How do you cook it?" This is so funny and yet so telling of the vast chasm between the country she left and where she found herself on that day.

In her village of Ramallah, waste was unheard of, and you certainly wouldn't water something you couldn't eat. From what I have been told by my Palestinian elders, roses were the exception. According to my parents, many families had roses in planters.

They enjoyed the beauty of the flowers, and they made rose water for the delectable Palestinian sweets like *Knafeh,* a mouthwatering layered dessert of shredded dough, soaked in rose and sugar syrup (*attar*) and filled with fresh sweet cheese and baked to a beautiful golden brown. Warm knafeh is a family favorite, and we rarely leave any Palestinian meal at a restaurant without getting some to go.

Many of the Tata activities were based on food, especially summertime when we would go to the local farms with the aunts, cousins, and their tatas. We would all pick the seasonal produce, whether it be tomatoes (*bandora*), squash (*kusa*), or okra (*bamiyeh*), and take our bounties home.

We would usually all then gather to clean, prep, and pack the vegetables in jars for the winter. After that, everyone would take home their share.

The jars would be placed in the basement cellar, and our eyes would come alive when we opened a jar of summer goodness in the dead of winter. This allowed us to enjoy our traditional dishes like stuffed squash *(mahshi)* all year long.

Our cellar had transom windows near the ceiling. By the end of summer, that cellar would be filled with so many jars, and when the sun was low in the sky and the cellar was filled with sunshine, those jars were aglow with the jewel colored goodness inside them.

This memory floods my senses every time I think of it. I used to love and sit in that cellar and admire that rainbow of our harvests.

Tata Zarifeh and I had some special moments we shared. One such pastime was to spend endless hours cracking walnuts together. We both enjoyed this very much, the cracking, the digging out the fresh walnut meats, and the eating as much as our bellies could tolerate. To this day, I find joy and comfort when cracking walnuts and keep a bowl on my kitchen counter.

I enjoyed her company very much; she reminded me a lot of her son, my dad, or vice versa, and I liked to take notice of their similarities. At the end of the day, I would love to tell my dad about the things I did with her.

Of course, dad loved his mother very much, and I remember that it was painful for him to watch her stumble with words and actions later in her life as she slipped into cognitive decline. One afternoon, I found my dad quietly sobbing in the family room. I said nothing and retreated to another room. I knew he had just returned from visiting his mom at her new assisted living facility for the first time. A few nights before, she had wandered out the front door into the street, confused and afraid. When he heard her walking in the hallway in the middle of the night, and then the front door closed, he got up to investigate and found her out front. After that, he and his siblings decided it was safest for her to be at the nursing home just down the street.

I am so grateful for the times I did have with her, especially when she was staying with us in our home. As I got older, I would help Tata with her bath and the braiding of her hair. She had a long wire wrapped with some sort of fabric that would be intertwined into her braid and looped back up to keep it all neat and tidy until the next bath, which happened every Saturday. She had had the wire for as long as I knew her. This once-weekly bath was a ritual from her Ramallah that she maintained in America. She especially loved it when I washed her back with the scratchy loofah. I enjoyed this practice very much, and throughout my life, I have enjoyed caring for the elderly.

For a time, I sang at old folks' homes with the Winifred Baker Chorale of San Francisco and cooked for elders at SF Hospice. An especially important person in my life was Irma Pedicini, who lived with us for a time when she was suffering from lung cancer, and whom I helped with showering and dressing daily. In many ways, she was a second grandmother to me. She was the grandmother of Paul Jordan, my 2nd husband. She taught me how to take my cooking skills to a new level and that less was more. She had a fiery spirit, and we loved each other very much. I miss her. I miss my Tata too. I imagine them in Heaven, along with the family they have there, almost certainly still holding court, as only they could do.

STORIES

Stories

When I think of stories from my childhood, there are two kinds of stories that come to mind: the ones told by my abundant and extended Palestinian family and the ones created by living my own life.

With so many relatives around who had fond memories of their comings and goings in the old country, hours and hours of storytelling were available to the story seeker. The seeking of storytelling has been a centerpiece in my life, and I hope that my children, grandchildren, and those who come after will take pleasure and guidance from the family stories.

It makes sense to me that an immigrant would possess a great desire to cherish and hold the stories of their country. I believe they told the stories to ensure that they remembered them as much as they wished to pass them on to the next generation to enjoy and to propel them forward.

I eagerly absorbed every story that every parent, aunt, uncle, cousin, and grandmother told. I remember sitting, listening, and then daydreaming that I was in the place and in the moment that they spoke of, trying with all my might to insert myself in the images of the world they were sharing.

By way of these stories, I was able to embed all those bits of Palestinian culture and ancestry into my life and ultimately into my way of thinking.

Mostly, the stories were for the adults, but I took what I could. The stories were filled with reflections of growing up in Ramallah and of the old ways that they still seemed to yearn for. They told happy stories of the best dishes and who made them. And they told many sad stories about the displacement of the Palestinians.

Despite so much hardship, my people thrived as their spirit was strong and unbroken. Loss and suffering was part of their story, their separation from country and home. This I know to be true because I recall the look in the eyes of these storytellers, a look of longing and of sadness, but there was much joy to share too. I believe it was their deep and intentional goal to keep the best parts of the life they left behind alive in their hearts and minds, for themselves and for their future generations.

Other stories were about what came next for them, which was the move to America. I loved the stories that my dad told me about coming to America, and especially about his early days in America. One of my favorite stories was the story of my dad when he was a traveling salesman and would go from farm to farm in Texas selling necessities to migrant workers.

He worked with his uncles' family and other new cousins in America. They sold textiles and other household necessities to people who needed them. From sunup to sundown, from farm to farm, packing their haul of goods every morning and hoping to have little to nothing left when they returned home utterly exhausted at the end of each day. This was before he went back home to Ramallah to be married to my mom and then to travel back to Detroit to start his new life in the auto industry as a husband and father. While he was back in Ramallah, he and my mom Jannette Dirbas were married, and also my big sister, Noel, was conceived.

My mom's stories of coming to America were quite different as she was a young female with her baby, little Noel, traveling across the sea on their own. She jokes about it as she tells her tale, and as much as she does not really say, it must have been terrifying.

Mom had a way about her that didn't allow much in the way of storytelling of the olden days. I am pretty certain that for Mom, talking about Ramallah brought her pain as she missed her family, all her friends, and the life she was forced to leave behind. Her marriage to my dad was arranged, so she had little choice in the matter of her future. And her future came so fast with the delivery of one daughter after the next. From 1954 to 1962, mom had four more girls! Busy she was with little time to ponder much, I imagine.

In the summer of 1962, my mom received terrible news. Her mother, our Tata Azizeh, passed away just before my youngest sister Michelle was born in August of 1962. After that, the few stories mom would tell were cloaked with a deep sadness, as telling them was now with the knowledge that she had left her mom behind, never to see her again, which must have been incredibly painful.

Storytelling was central to our kitchen chores and to our gatherings and was usually sprinkled with some fresh gossip. Every day the women and girls listened along while the men enjoyed their coffee (*kahwah*), sometimes just our immediate family but more often than not relatives were present too. It was the state of life for gatherings to be as big as possible and for everyone to ultimately be surrounded with as much connection to Ramallah as possible, the more of us there were the more the home they left behind was accessible through the stories everyone would tell but mostly because they embodied the essence of that home.

In the evenings, we had our tea, and sometimes we had stories. Reading stories in books was not something we did much of in my childhood. Not that I recall anyway. The books that I remember in our home were the shiny, brand-new World Book Encyclopedia set that my father purchased when I was a child. I remember daddy being so proud of his encyclopedia purchase. He would take one book at a time and read it from front to back. That's how he was. He knew about so many things, and I always attribute it to his incredible sense of wonder and thirst for knowledge, and to those encyclopedias.

I smile when I remember seeing him pick the next encyclopedia up from his alphabetical A-Z lineup and take it with him to the restroom for a good read. Since following my father's footsteps guided my childhood, it held true here as well, and so I spent many hours with my face buried in those books. I think both of us may have a short attention span, and to some degree, I believe that's why these books and the Reader's Digest had such appeal to us. Little snippets of education, and then on to the great activities and work of the day. I still have these books as they were a centerpiece in our home. These encyclopedias became the source for many a story. Dad would go on and on telling us what he learned from A-Z. I loved all of those stories too!

The storytelling that I got to experience in childhood may have been partly due to the fact that we didn't have many other books when we were kids. If we did, I didn't notice them, or I didn't care about them. My guess is that whatever books we had, being shared by three, then four, then five girls, I didn't have much access, or maybe I simply wasn't that interested.

I think about the common threads in the stories of the old days that were told to us children: perseverance, kindness, resourcefulness, and joy, all weaving together to tell the true story of my people. And when I think about all I read in those encyclopedias, I came to know that there was the world I lived in, and there was a much wider world waiting out there for me to experience.

Daddy, Mommy & Noel & me on the way.
Michigan early 1954

WORK

Work

The best boss I ever had was my father. I worked with him in our grocery stores from a young age and on and off until we moved to San Francisco in 1972. During that time, I learned so much from him.

Dad allowed my older sister, Noel, and me to go to the store and help with random jobs, mostly in the back stock room. We put away lots of old glass soda pop bottles in little wooden crates when people returned them for the bottle refund. Pop, as we called it, was immensely popular in Michigan when I grew up. We had to separate all the bottles: Nehi orange soda, 7-Up, Coca-Cola, Vernor's root beer, to name a few. We were even allowed, rather expected, to separate the stinky beer bottles that customers returned.

I can still remember the smell of those used bottles to this day. I also remember how sticky my hands would get after handling them. When I think back on this job, I get grossed out by how absolutely disgusting and germ-ridden it was, but we didn't know any better. I hope I washed my hands after that chore. Maybe not, who knows after all, we were just kids. I could never imagine asking my children to do such a job, but times are different for sure.

Noel and I got this job, among others, because my father said he needed more help at the store. We were happy to help because it was fun, and like I said, I thought it was thrilling and so interesting to be at the store with him. Soon after we became adept at this bottle task, we were promoted to receiving the grocery load off the big delivery truck and then placing the cases of goods in their respective aisles for shelving. We had a complete aisle number marking system down in the large back room. Dad had taped the aisle numbers on the cement floor, and then Noel and I would place the boxes in the aisle number that corresponded with where that product would be located on the shelf. I really liked this part of our job. I felt so proud of our knowledge and ability to help Dad.

Once the cases were set in the right aisle, we would have to open the boxes and hand price every product. In those days, we had a push-down ink marker, a clunky metal gadget that had an ink reservoir for the ink pad at the bottom and rotating numbers at the top.

We would have to rotate the numbers on the marker to the retail that dad had written on the box of product, or to match what was on the shelf. We would then price the cans and boxes before placing them on the shelves. Another messy, dirty job that left us with inky hands and clothes. My big sister and I did all manner of other jobs in the store that consisted of so many random little jobs, but always lots of dusting, cleaning, and facing of the shelves. All the boxes and cans had to be just perfectly lined up on the shelves and facing forward.

One of my favorite parts of the day was when the morning bakery deliveries would arrive, and dad would let us pick a pastry, and he would have one too. He loved the Archway brand of iced spiced cakes, and I loved the coconut snowballs. This consisted of a domed chocolate sponge cake that had a fluffy white cream injected into the center, and then the entire dome was covered with a blanket of sweet coconut confection. There were two of these in each package. Breakfast of champions it was not, but who cared in those days. I don't remember ever hearing that something was not good for us. On the other hand, we consumed so much healthy home-cooked Palestinian food, and that was certainly the majority of what we ate so that more than made up for the few highly processed treats. I often think about what mom and dad must have thought about the hundreds of new foods that they experienced when they came to America. Processed foods were probably near nonexistent in Ramallah in those days.

Working in a retail environment has great value and offers many learning opportunities. When that business is family-owned by a newcomer to America, from my perspective, the value increases tenfold. The social interactions, the various vendors and patrons, the customer service, and the moment-to-moment variation of transactions all served as teachable moments.

I always felt that my ability to think on my feet and adapt to most situations stemmed from the exposure I had in our stores. Watching my dad navigate the early years as a self-made businessman in America was staggering, if not wildly entertaining.

I also enjoyed separating coins and anything to do with the register. Once I was able to ring up the customers, I became familiar with many of our regulars, and that's where I met my next employer, the dentist up the road from our store. He would stop at our store almost every day on his way home. When he was checking out at our store, sometimes I would ask him about what it was like to be a dentist. Maybe he thought I wanted to be a dentist someday, and before I knew it, he asked me if I could help him and his wife, Marge, at the dental office. Working for the dentist is when I got my first paycheck, and then every week after that, more money came. It felt so liberating to have my very own money.

Asking lots of questions was my way. I know I was never afraid to ask questions; in fact, my dad used to tease me that I "came out asking questions." I remember on more than one occasion, my dad would say, "Stop asking so many questions!"

As an adult, so many years later, the love of my life, John, always likes to say that I am an "information-seeking missile."

That always makes me laugh, and I only wish that my dad were here to hear him say that.

Of course, I had absolutely zero training in anything related to a dental office, but I was so excited about what felt like a big adventure. On day one in that dental office, it became obvious to me that working with my dad had taught me so many skills that I put to immediate use there. Customer service, organization, math, administration, and general operational duties. In fact, those skills and many more served as a strong foundation that has guided me throughout my life and career, and even those early days at the dental office.

At the dentist's office. I worked with children to show them how to clean and floss their teeth. There was a sweet little children's room in the office where they could learn about their teeth and oral hygiene. I would show them how to look through a microscope at the bacteria that I would scrape off their teeth. As they looked through the microscope, they could see all the bacteria (little bugs as we called them) playing on their teeth, creating cavities. Then I would explain that this was why it was so important that the bacteria be carefully removed by way of brushing and flossing. I can still remember the look on their faces and the little screams they made when they saw those little jiggling bugs.

Once, when the certified dental assistant was away on holiday, and I was filling in, taking care of random things, Dr. H had to do an emergency denture. Since no one else was there, I had to assist, and it was horrifying, to say the least. If I tried to describe it here, you would be horrified too, but I survived and so did the patient.

I quickly became responsible for bookkeeping, locking up the office, filling all the supplies, and any number of dental office tasks. It was way too much responsibility for a 16-year-old, and I remember driving back there more than once to confirm that I had truly locked the doors. I'm sure a little OCD played a part in this as well.

Once, Dr. H and his wife, Marge, invited me to a party at their home. This was to be my first glimpse into the glamorous life that a doctor sometimes lives. I remember walking around their property, home, and garden, and feeling overwhelmed by the beautiful aesthetic and furniture, and especially all the art. I hadn't seen anything like that before. He was such a humble man, and I did not expect the lavish surroundings and bountiful offerings of food and drink. I remember going home and telling my mom all about it.

Another odd job I had while I was in High School was working at a model home business office across the street from our grocery store. These model homes were beautiful, brand new, and quite modern, and were replicas of new homes available to purchase in Florida. Lots of folks in Michigan liked to travel to Florida for the winters or during retirement.

These models were unlike any homes I had ever seen, and so was the gorgeous mid-century furniture. Potential purchasers would come to see them and look at land maps of developments in Miami or Fort Lauderdale. I was there to answer questions as best I could but mostly get names and phone numbers so that the agents could call them back.

When I was bored, I would run across the street to our store and grab a couple of snacks and run back. In my short absences, I kept watch for anyone driving up to the homes. I would have my snacks, hang out, and look at magazines to pass the time while I waited for people who came in to search for their Florida dream house. That was an easy job with tasty benefits and the unbridled freedom to hang out and look at magazines without a parent or sister looking over my shoulder.

Soon after we moved to California, which is where I got my next quite wacky job. I took a temporary holiday position at Hickory Farms. I loved making their famous holiday cheese balls there in South San Francisco. The entire shift, all I had to do was make those cheese balls. I still love those cheesy orbs with a cherry on top. There were buckets of processed and somewhat creamy cheddar cheese that I would form into a perfect ball. From there each one was weighed and then rolled in chopped nuts, weighed again and the adorned with a maraschino cherry. They were quite popular in their day, but that job ended at the end of the year.

Later in California, I worked for a dentist in Millbrae and then one off of West Portal in San Francisco and another one a few years later in Marin County.

I even got my X-ray technician license when I worked for Dr. S in San Francisco near West Portal soon after I became a newlywed in 1974. He drove a fancy red Thunderbird. His image is memorable as he was tall, thin, with slick back dark hair just like in the movie "Grease," and he always wore white socks and shiny black loafers. I also keenly recall that he rarely spoke to anyone, and I found that so disturbing. Thank goodness for his wonderful office manager, Olga as she and I became quick friends.

Olga came from Russia to San Francisco with her family when she was 10 years old and was raising a young son on her own.

Olga and her son Michael lived in Parkmerced near San Francisco State University. My new husband, Jerry Harb, and I ended up moving there, too. We shared a common backyard space where we would sometimes meet and have lunch on the lawn.

When we were working together, she used to invite me to lunch at her parents' home in the Sunset district, and we would eat borscht, bread, and cheese. Her parents were lovely and so welcoming. The familiar Orthodox icons that hung in the home were so beautiful, familiar, and comforting.

We had some things in common, one being that she was Russian Orthodox, and we were Antiochian Orthodox, and we celebrated some of the Orthodox holidays together. I so enjoyed learning about all of the Russian holiday specialties. It was so special to have such a friend where I worked.

Of all the dentists, though, my favorite was Dr. B in Millbrae. His office was just down the hill from one of our first homes in California.

When I think back on all my bosses, he always treated me with kindness, respect, and as an equal. Every other boss I think of was sometimes disrespectful or condescending, sometimes unkind, and even unprofessional. I always felt this was due to gender and maybe even cultural biases.

I have always had to be tougher, smarter, and more productive to make a place for myself in the workplace. As hard as I tried, I believe I could have done much more at an earlier age to forge my way and assert myself in more meaningful ways if I had known how to do so.

Possessing these skills and self-awareness is where the power lies. Without the knowledge of what is possible or the maturity to recognize your options, you can't quite reach that power. As a young girl, I was raised to know my female place and not cause a scene or be disrespectful to men and elders, so for me, this made it difficult to hold my own and speak up when I felt I was being mistreated. I believed at that time, and now, to a lesser degree, I still believe things are harder for women. Over time, there has been change, but I will always hope for a time when everyone is equal and the only defining characteristic is that we are all human. Work is work, and for the most part, we all do our best to get the job done.

But as the stars would have it, the job of office work and monitoring oral hygiene were not my passion… but I already knew that. It was at a time in my life as a teenager, then a newlywed and young mother, when I just needed steady work and money.

I woke up one day with my small children and realized that I needed to do something different. The stories, traditions, and foods of my young life captured my imagination and seeped into my soul. They grabbed hold of me in such a way that made the sharp contrast of these things to dental jobs feel like I was watching a movie that was badly cast, with me as the main character. I was about to embark on what was the real second act to my career, the first act, of course, being dad's helper at the store not the making of cheese balls nor the dental office bits.

The entrepreneurial spirit moved in me, and I came to

realize that I wanted to be my own boss like my dad, and work with people and food, and so I did.

A small deli came up for sale in San Bruno, CA, and with dad's help, I was able to buy it. This was the way it started. A sandwich shop and Deli that I named Harb's Deli, and from there grew to two more delis in San Francisco called Out To Luch, where catering became a large segment of the business.

I can't say enough about growing up the way I did and how it taught me to be self-reliant, open-minded, and comfortable in various situations. I learned a lot about determination and finishing what you start. I also learned a lot about thinking on your feet and being adaptable. This might be my nature, but I am confident that those years working with my dad and also with my mother at home instilled sensibilities for which I am grateful. The things I learned from each of my parents fill the deepest of wells, and it is my hope that my children and grandchildren will think the same of me.

Each of my children, Elise, and Jameel, has expressed to me their profound appreciation for some of what they have learned from me. After earning his law degree, Jameel told me that he thinks one of the reasons he was finding success at work and in life is that he has that same ability to think on his feet. I remember how good I felt to hear him tell me that. Mostly, the deep sense of accomplishment and happiness that I heard in his voice is what I carry with me. Watching Elise with her children is the most amazing and absolute acknowledgment of what she took with her from her childhood home and into her own home. The beauty of this cycle of paying it forward with family is a most precious gift.

The result of my children's skills and tenacious ways has given them full and successful lives and paying witness to this unfold over the decades has been one of my greatest joys. The best job I will ever hold in life is that of being a mother, for which there is no paycheck, but so many unquantifiable bonuses, rewards, and promotions, like being promoted to *Tayta*. (This is our word for grandmother. I spell mine with a Y in the middle. Others say Tata, Tete, Tate ... so many variations.

The rest of my life was filled with decades of work in the grocery business and with producers, either as an employee or a consultant.

In 2000, John and I started a consultancy business working with retail specialty markets and manufacturers. We had met four years earlier and left that company and started our business together. We both knew we would make great partners, and we did, both in business and later in life. This new venture was real work every day, all day, but I enjoyed it. Working with people and food made sense to me. We were good at it, and we made a difference for our clients. It's quite satisfying to create ideas, opportunities, and tangible results. We have been consulting for 25 years with manufacturers and independent grocers. We have supported all aspects of this business, including new stores and remodels, hiring and training, product development, procurement, and analysis. We still find challenge, satisfaction, and fun in our work together.

While my father was alive, I loved speaking to him almost daily. I would call him from California on my drives between markets, and many times we would talk about the grocery business. He was always interested in what I was working on. He was my ally, and I always knew he was keenly interested and often had great suggestions. He asked me lots of questions. He was my first boss, and we always had the grocery business in common.

My sister Elizabeth and I shared that as well. She married a family in Pennsylvania that was in the same business. She was super smart, quite conservative, and would have been a great CFO. She was able to share these strengths to bring increased profitability to the family business. After dad passed away, I still had Liz to talk business with, and I always loved that we shared a similar career.

So, now so many years later I find myself thinking about not working. As I approached 70 and retirement, or most likely semi-retirement, I think about all the things I plan to do and feel relieved to recognize that I have been doing all the things I wanted to do, all along.

I have tried not to let work get in the way of enjoying life to the fullest. Money comes and money goes, and I have always worked hard so that I could have as much freedom to live my best life and to fill it with adventure and wonder.

I don't take this for granted, though, and I thank my parents regularly for having the courage and tenacity to create a wonderful life for us here in America and for giving me my start in business.

Maybe they wanted a different choice; maybe they wished they could have stayed in Ramallah, but here they were, and they worked hard and brought so much joy and bounty into our lives and so many others' lives. I told them many times how grateful I was to have the opportunities they gave me and ultimately gave my children.

It is true that the human condition brings an innate drive to care for and protect your loved ones, and I would have done the same, but in the end, they were the ones who made the difficult and risk-laden journey from there to here.

As a first-generation child, sometimes I feel a twinge of guilt that I was able to benefit so deeply from all that they gave up to raise their family with freedoms and securities that no longer existed where they were.

I wonder what they thought of it as they looked back over the many decades that came after those first years. The early work, especially of building a new life, must have been so challenging, day after day, and loaded with so many unknowns. It offered many rewards, too, in spite of daily obstacles, including racism and bias, which were an everyday part of life. They overcame this and proudly lived their lives, and we girls did the same.

My hard-working and deeply loving parents will remain my heroes through eternity.

MOM

Mom

My mom has always been larger than life and full of energy. She was a force as a young mother, and in her 90s, she still is. I have many wonderful memories of my mother, as do my sisters and pretty much everyone, because she has always left indelible imprints on everyone she came in contact with.

She was full of life, but at times she seemed full of longing, too.

Many of these memories are from my childhood, as far back as what I believe to be three years old, when we lived in Detroit. One particular memory was me sitting on the arm of the sofa, and her scolding me to get down because I would fall. Like many mothers, she had eyes in the back of her head. I remember this incredible trait of hers well, as she always knew everything that was going on all around her. She saw everything, she heard everything, and she smelled everything too. We all talked about her ability to smell everything long before anyone else could; this special sensory talent that she possessed.

By the time I was three, my mom had two girls and another one on the way. Mom was having child after child, what turned out to be daughter after daughter. The five daughters, Noel, Patricia, Sharon, Elizabeth, and Michele, are all two to two and a half years apart. That's a lot of activity in 10 years, and I am still awestruck when I think of it. She really was tough to the core. Hard as nails, I always say, and I can never imagine doing what she did and enduring what she endured.

To raise such a large family even under more normal

circumstances would be a feat in itself. My mother started her motherhood adventure across continents and then continued far from her native home, and yet she always did it with much style, yes, even panache, and always intense pride.

Mom had her first child in Palestine and traveled solo to America with her new baby in tow. That little girl, my big sister Noel, is the only one of us who has the distinction of being born in Palestine because mom had the rest of us in America, in Michigan specifically.

My mother always loved nice clothes and lovely things. Coming to America gave her a treasure trove of opportunities to spend money with little to no impunity. She always wanted the best things, and once my father started earning a good living, and with his subsequent successes with the stores, my mother's cash flow was endless. In her mind, anyway.

We have many pictures of mom in various stages of pregnancy and always looking perfect in her very stylish attire and perfectly coiffed hair. Every Saturday, without exception, she would go to the salon to have her hair done. As the years rolled on, I came to recognize that all my aunts and all the other Palestinian ladies dyed their hair the exact same shade of medium auburn. One time before a wedding, I went to see Rima, as it was customary for the young girls in our community to treat every big event like a cotillion of sorts, showing off their beauty and coming of age to the relatives. Rima was a cousin who became a hairstylist and came with a built-in patronage of Ramallah ladies. She worked out of her basement and was a wonderfully kind and on-trend woman who was easy to talk to. I like her very much and admire her natural beauty and later came to learn that it was her entrepreneurship and independence that excited me most.

I was comfortable with Rima, so I asked her about this one color of dye. Why on earth did all the aunts dye their hair the same color?

She asked me to follow her, so I got up from the chair, and she showed me where all her hair dye was, and there were only bottles of that one color. When we got back to the chair, I asked the question again and she just looked at me via the mirror in front of us and said, 'you know our ladies, they all want what the other has'. This was mostly true at the time.

I believe this discovery informed me of my decision to let my hair go gray naturally. I tried a hair color once or twice; it wasn't that dark auburn, and still, the false color was not for me.

Not only did my mother dress to the nines, but she also kept her girls perfectly dressed and maintained. I remember Easter Sunday when each of us had a new dress, bonnet, and shoes, and even coordinated bags and gloves. We would all be lined up by dad's newest car, where a photo was taken. I remember as an adult watching the miniseries Mad Men and thinking about my mom and how much the women's clothing and hairdos of that era brought back memories of how she looked in the late 50's and early 60's. My dad didn't have as much of an opportunity to dress up as he was mostly in the grocery store, but my mom made certain that he always looked "sharp" for any festivity.

Frankly, I don't think he cared a lick about nice clothes. He was extremely happy in his everyday work clothes and slippers as often as he was allowed to wear them.

Mom always looking so lovely even on days when she was cooking and cleaning while trying to corral five daughters. My children's other Tata, Jean Harb, was also very glamorous at all times. How does this happen? I certainly did not look glamorous when I was raising my children. In the end, I have decided that some people care a lot more about their clothing and appearance than others. I always say that my children got their great sense of style from their Tatas. Frankly, clothes were functional for me, and I was not motivated to spend money on a showy wardrobe. Nor did I want to spend an hour getting ready for the day; I just wanted the day to start and to get going. I did not want to miss any of the good stuff that might be happening outside.

We all had many good days with mom hanging around the house and yard, helping in the kitchen, visiting with aunts and cousins, going on picnics or to the farms, and all of the other lovely, idyllic moments of childhood.

Mom was always go, go, go, so much to do and so little time. She didn't drive in those days, so whenever she could rustle up a ride from one of her relatives, we were off and running, usually to the mall. When we were quite young, we didn't have to go to the grocery stores much, as mom always had a list of things she asked Dad to bring home from the store. Poor dad, he hated when he got that list late after a long day of work, and then still had to go through the aisles and pick up everything on that list. To make it worse, when he got home and mom was unpacking the groceries, he certainly heard about any single item that was not to her liking. Of course, mom wanted the best and freshest of everything, and he wanted to bring home things that might have been close-dated or otherwise unlikely to sell. This was a constant tug of war between them. I used to love to be creative and make things with the random, unlabeled tin cans he would bring home. That was fun. My best creation was when I opened a can of spam, a can of peas, and a can of pears. I made a summer salad of these items, adding Hellman's mayo and diced green onions. My dad loved that salad, and so did I. Mom refused to try it and said something like, "who wants to eat that garbage." Mom had a way with words. She said whatever popped into her brain, unfiltered, to say the least at all times.

As time went on and we started to get a little older, there were more and more days when my mother was about to lose her mind with five girls running around, and my dad being busy at the store or at the race tracks. On these days, I remember mom chasing us around with her slippers or yelling at the top of her lungs tearing at her house dress or blouse that we needed to come in. She would get so angry when we didn't listen that I thought she might faint. I don't remember her ever spanking us, although inevitably it must have happened.

We would play in the basement and my mother would call us for lunch or to do some chores; several moments later after being ignored, she would bolt down the stairs with her slippers slapping against her heels and her gold bracelets jingling and jangling all the way down and we knew that she was after us!

We all went running towards various hiding places in the basement, laughing the entire time. My sisters and I can easily recall the alarming sound of slippers and bangles as she came for us. Noel, Sharon, and I for sure anyway.

That basement has lots of mom stories. I remember helping my mom wash boxes of large green olives from the Eastern Market. She washed them in the washing machine! I remember so vividly that sound of those big tumbling and thumping olives. They got clean, and my mom was incredibly pleased with her ingenuity.

The basement was our prep area where anything too dirty for the upstairs kitchen took place. One example is when we washed the lamb intestines there. The smell was terrible, but after helping my mom turn each intestine inside out, and after so many washes and soakings, they were sparkling clean. A pot of stuffed grape leaves (*Warak*) layered with the stuffed lamb intestines is a masterpiece, but I can understand that not everyone reading this will agree. If you can get past the idea of it, I promise you will find it superb and worth all that work.

Once on the way to that basement, I fell down that whole flight of stairs. On a tray, I was carrying down pop bottles and a snack to enjoy with my sisters and some cousins, and the worn edge of my sneakers caught the edge of the stairs, and that was the last thing I remember as I went tumbling down. The next thing I see is my mother's face above me, holding tweezers and gently removing pieces of glass from my face and arm. My Tata Zarifeh was there too. I can still remember the look and tears in my momma's eyes when she was helping me, and in that moment, I felt calm and safe under their watchful eyes and tender care. I have a few scars that have become barely visible with the healing of decades and the addition of wrinkles.

Another especially lovely memory of my mother was when I was taking a bath around age six, and my mother was kneeling outside the bathtub with the sponge, smiling at me in the most soothing way, and squeezing the warm water from the sponge over my head repeatedly. She didn't have a ton of time for these one-on-one exchanges, so I relished them when they came my way.

I can only imagine how challenging her day-to-day world was in those days. Her support group was really mostly my aunt Azizeh Aneed, and then my aunt Suad George when they came from the old country. These ladies made my mother's world much more bearable. I have many memories of my mom relaxing on the chair, gossiping with one of them, talking about what they were going to make for dinner, and how much they paid for various cuts of meat, clothing, or whatever the shopping experience of the day was. I really enjoyed listening. I found this female chatter so comforting.

Other favorite experiences and memories of my mom have to do with my mother's incredible appetite for books. I remember watching her read as probably the most singular indicator of her calm interludes. I would sometimes sit near where she was reading and listen to her breathing. My mom suffered from allergies when we lived in Michigan, and sometimes when she would rub her nose or her ears, the jangling of her bracelets would be the only other sound as she lay on the couch with her face buried in those pages.

Sometimes I would pick up her books to try to read what she was reading, and I can tell you this, my mother loved a good love story.

My two favorite aunts, Azizeh and Suad, were incredible cooks and I think it was the central motivation for my mother's amazing food. At some point in my young life, maybe around eleven, my mom had achieved the honor of top chef in our world. I have never tasted Palestinian food better than my mother's. If you think about it and consider the amazingly huge number of Palestinian dishes I've eaten at all my cousins' homes, her being referred to as 'the best' by so many is a big deal. I'm fairly sure all of my sisters and many of my cousins and aunts (most of the aunts) would agree, and certainly the uncles. She had an incredibly insatiable appetite to be the best cook in our community, and she succeeded.

In 1972, the whole family moved to California to be closer to dad's brothers, Mousa, Fuad, and Nabil, his mom, and two of his sisters, Yasmin and Mary.

Now with five daughters in tow, my mom had to make another massive life change. This was a difficult but exciting period in all our lives, to be sure. My mom had to cope with each daughter's own set of complaints, fears, and anxieties about moving cross country and leaving everything they knew, along with her own feelings and concerns. Mom was making a critical shift to suddenly be living around Dad's side of the family instead of her own. Everything in her daily routine would be different from what it was. She no longer would have the comfort of a sibling stopping by on a daily basis. This move also meant mom lost a favorite pastime of hers; to chatter about this and that or the incredible deal she got on a recent Coach handbag with her sister Siham and her sister in law Salwa. The constant hum of sibling arguments in her family room would be gone. She was to find herself in a new world that was quite far removed from the second home she came to know in Livonia, Michigan. Heading even further west now, to California, offered many new things. This time though, she traveled with her jumbo family of seven instead of solo with her firstborn.

Together, we all navigated our way through the uncharted waters of living in California with much more of our dad's family instead of our mom's. It all came together with so much to do every day to get settled into home, school, and work. We had many good years in California with each daughter getting married, one by one, and then sadly three of my sisters moving away.

After all the weddings had been planned and attended, and most of her grandbabies were born, another move was inevitable.

In 1986, just fourteen years later my mom and dad moved back to Michigan. The cost of living was much lower, and they would be closer to more family again. The financial burdens that living in California had created were becoming significant as well.

Another painful factor was that by that time; my poor dad had lost his mom to Alzheimer's disease and all three of his brothers and one of his sisters to heart disease. In the end, I know he was grateful to have spent that precious time with all of them in California for as long as he could. So much happened during those fourteen years in California.

Years later, when my father became ill and my mother ultimately became his caretaker, she devoted her days and nights to his comfort. My father used to say that she was an angel and speak adoringly of how incredibly lucky he was. Even though she would nag and criticize him endlessly at times, he still worshipped her. I believe he understood her and was amazed by how brilliant my mother was. He respected her stamina and tenacious approach to getting things done.

Now that my mom is older and needs care, we are there for her. She gave us all so much. She wasn't perfect, and even when she was 100% wrong about something she said or something she did, I never heard her apologize. This was not in her playbook, but her love was constant and intense.

My mother is, in fact, brilliant; she always loved to learn, and she wanted to have the answers. It helps, too, that she has an incredible memory. My mother remembered everything in those days before dementia started to set in. So much so that her daughters have had to ask her about things that have happened in the past because she certainly remembered more than most of us. My son Jameel has this gift of memory as well. I've always thought that folks with the best memories seem smarter because they remember everything they ever learned. Around age 85, my mom began to show the early signs of dementia, and this was so difficult, especially for her, as she was always so proud of her ability to share stories and information and set the record straight about what really happened.

There was always so much competition between mom and her siblings about who was right, just about anything. My sisters and I could each share stories about the barrage of arguments we witnessed when they started challenging one another about some random incident or price at the store, or brand that was best. It was really endless, annoying but dear in it's own way. This is how that family wove their stories and showed their love for each other.

Mom is such an amazing woman. I knew as a child that she was a force...and gratefully, as I write this, and even with declining cognition and health, she still tries to tell us how it is, how it was, and how it should be.

Mom on the left and her brother Sami to her right with friends in Ramallah

Mom and her five girls. Me at the top right.

Mom on the balcony. I was on the balcony next door taking this picture. We were on a Cruise to Puerto Rico August 2008. Catching her smile always made me smile.

Mom with all her daughters and my daughter, Elise. November 11, 2013, Savannah, Georgia, for Mom's 80th Birthday

FRIEND

Friend

I did not like being in high school and felt like an outcast, and as a result, I kept to myself. Maybe it was my own doing, but I certainly didn't feel like I fit in. There were two groups of kids; on one side, it was the hippie mod types, and on the other side were the traditionalists, who mostly came from monied families and were very 'rah-rah' and followed all the rules. I did not feel welcome or connected to either side. There were a few kids on the hippie side that I wanted to get to know, but when I tried, I never got far.

It was the late 60's and early 70's and rebellion was in the air. The entire experience of high school was awkward and caused me stress. It was more than teenage angst; it felt foreign and unwelcoming.

There was one girl, Karen, who lived up the street from us on Ellen Drive. She and I became great friends at the beginning of high school. She came from a family that seemed atypical and far less traditional than the other white families I saw around.

Just like my family, they seemed different than all the other families in the neighborhood. Her parents were very liberal and allowed Karen total freedom. I was drawn to that because our Palestinian family was quite different in that regard. Neither of our families seemed to be great fits within this seemingly snobby neighborhood. I say that because many of those neighbors didn't even say hello and were not welcoming in any way when I walked around the neighborhood. I would wave and say hi, and they would just ignore me. Sometimes, I got a long stare up and down as though they were summing up my attire and maybe the color of my skin. I would hear mom tell the same stories, too.

But Karen was different, and so was her family. She and I hit it off, and we spent a lot of time together. We both saw ourselves as free spirits and loved nature, music, art, and food. We would spend our time together walking in the woods, listening to music, writing poetry, and drawing. Karen would tell me stories of her escapades, and I would sit and listen in fascination. She loved the boys and was able to come and go as she pleased, heading out after dinner to meet a boy and coming home late. I, on the other hand, was allowed to do no such thing.

Karen was very independent and a bit of a rabble rouser. She did as she pleased, and that was the opposite of my world.

We would do girly spa things like braiding our long hair while wet, letting it dry while we put on face masks. Then we would unravel our braids and enjoy our suddenly wavy hair, looking so cool and mod. We would listen to music while talking about all the things we want to do in life or next week. As soon as I graduated from high school, our family moved to California, but Karen and I stayed in touch, and a couple of times when I've gone back to Michigan, we got together. One time she came to visit in California and stayed with me in San Rafael with her family. It felt strange and familiar at the same time. She was happily married, and I was divorced and living on my own for the first time in my life. How things change. She had always enjoyed the freedoms of life and now that I had my own freedom it felt overwhelming to experience that for the first time in my early 40's.

We are still friends to this day, although our interactions

have diminished over the years. Like all great friends, every time we talk, we say how it seems like it was just yesterday that we were doing scary things like running through the golf course during thunderstorms.

After Karen got married, she moved to the Upper Peninsula of Michigan and became a nurse practitioner and has an incredible reputation in her profession. She lives on a large property with its own lake, and they farm and have a way of life that she always wanted.

My experience was that Karen was very liberal and a naturalist, living her Bohemian lifestyle. After many school crushes and a few heady experiences, I am sure that she married the love of her life and had her two sons. In our own ways, we were both rebels and did not want to follow the written path, but in the end, we pretty much did what parents expect us to do, which was to get married and have children.

Karen and I saw eye to eye, and she coveted the unusual that she found in our family, and I coveted her incredible freedom and her wild and eccentric mom. We've laughed about that often. We enjoyed sharing stories about my Palestinian culture, our traditions, our upbringing, and the trials and tribulations with our families, whatever they were.

In the end, we found our shared experience brought light and laughter to our heady and sometimes overwhelming teenage days.

Life is full of the strange and beautiful moments, and I shared some of my favorite teenage times with Karen. I do believe in kindred spirits and that we are so blessed when we find one.

I reminisce often about when we both took our sketch pads and pencils to Park Lawn Cemetery in Livonia, which was close to home.

Karen and I used to go there to draw and just sit under the trees. It is strange to think about those days now, knowing that I was walking around where my father is now buried and where my momma will be buried next to daddy one day. Sitting on the lawn, and drawing pictures, and never imagining in a million years that they would rest here one day along with so many members of their families.

All the aunts and uncles who helped to raise me, who taught me to cook, and my father, and mother; the beautiful collection of humans who helped me become me.

Karen loved that cemetery too, and I like to think that when she drives by, she thinks about her Palestinian family just around the corner. When we talk, even 50 years later, we still enjoy sharing stories about the same subjects. When it comes to friends, I always say it's not quantity but quality. Karen was truly my only real friend throughout school, someone that I sought out and nurtured a relationship with.

I remember a couple of girls that I saw a couple of times, but I didn't think they understood our household and how different it was from theirs, and that would be the end of the relationship. I had parents who looked different than theirs, foods that looked, smelled, and tasted different than theirs too. Hearing an unusual language being spoken may have been just too much for some. The unfamiliar created an unease that was palpable. After a few of these exchanges with other girls in my neighborhood, when walking past their house, if any of the family was out front, I could feel the curiosity and even judgment out in the suburbs of Detroit where we lived. I thought that was so strange that just a few miles away in Dearborn was the largest Arab population in the country and yet here in Livonia, at that time, it was a world away.

When I was younger, there were many neighborhood kids that we played with, but I can't think of any true friends that I had during my school years, except Karen, and that was ok with me. I had plenty of sisters and cousins, and that was enough. Cousins are the most amazing friends after all, and sisters...well, let's just say that each one is a blessing and for completely different reasons and for all the same reason.

And now I have one best friend and that is Siobain. She is my dearest friend and one that I have known since 1990. She is like a sister to me. The times we have spent together are some of my fondest treasures. She has a heart that is so vast and a lust for life that is contagious. My family thinks of her as family, and we would go to the ends of the universe for each other. I have known her for half of my life, and I cherish the past, present, and future days with her. We have shared joyful and difficult times, marriages, and divorces, each the death of a parent, and so much more. A friend of childhood has such a different landscape than a friend of adulthood has. The seasons of life bring just the right kind of friend to you if you are paying attention.

There are friends, there is family, and there are the friends that become family.

DRIVE

Drive

I learned to drive in my older sister's Dodge Dart, which I was allowed to use. I don't know where Dad got it; it just appeared one day.

As one might imagine, I was wildly excited. It was pale yellow and perfect, for a few days anyways, as it didn't take me long to put a couple of dents in that Dart.

I remember wishing I could have a green Carmen Ghia, as I loved those adorable, oddly shaped cars. They looked so strange and suited my sensibilities about being different and not blending in. Since my father worked in the car factories of Detroit, it was unlikely we would get anything but an American-made car. My father respected the industry that ultimately gave him the opportunity for a new home and all he needed for his growing family. He would tell us a lot of stories about his role there, the assembly line projects, and promotions he quickly received. As much as he wanted to and eventually did attain his independence and own his own business, he had a great sense of pride for what he did on those lines. I know they were lucky to have him, and I think in some ways it boosted his entrepreneurial spirit to a higher level of confidence. He was always in the driver's seat about what was coming next. He always had a determination, a drive to be successful.

I didn't drive to high school very often until my senior year. I do recall using the Dart or whichever other car we had at the time to run errands for my mom and to go to our store, Meadowland Market.

My first little fender bender happened when I was heading to the store to help dad. I was about to make a left turn, but I missed doing it before the light turned from yellow to red. I was so nervous; panicked, really, and thought I should just back up behind the crosswalk, then be sure to hit the gas when it was my turn before the oncoming cars arrived. Well, that didn't work out as planned. The problem was that I forgot to put it back in drive, and as soon as the light turned green, I floored the gas and ran into the car behind me. It was so terrible and frightening, and I thought I'd be in huge trouble. I remember walking to the corner liquor store and calling my father, who came from the store a few blocks away to rescue me.

After that incident, I wasn't eager to drive, but of course, I eventually got over it. I can see my dad's face still, the way he looked at me with a crooked smile that said both I love you and be more careful. He never said a word, but my mom had lots to say about it.

Another memorable car story happened when I went to run an errand. I pulled out of the garage, headed down the driveway, realized I forgot something, and quickly pulled back into the garage. After retrieving what I needed, I was on my way. As I drove down the service drive, I noticed people waving at me (what I thought was a wave) and how friendly everyone was. It wasn't just one or two that passed me but every single person that passed. To be polite, I waved back, of course. About a mile from home, someone tried to flag me down. That's when I realized something must be wrong with my car. I got out, walked around to the front, and there it was, the big old style basket grass catcher attached to my front license plate! I figured it must've gotten caught when I pulled into the garage and got too close to the wall where the basket was sitting.

I thought about all the people who saw me driving with

that grass catcher hanging from my license plate and was so embarrassed, I decided I wouldn't drive again for a while. I wondered how many people had recognized me.

I had a few more mishaps, but all in all, I believe I became a good driver, but that might depend on who you ask.

A first car has so much to offer a young person. Playing the radio as loud as I wanted was a highlight. The freedom to drive around was heavenly, but I learned quickly that driving also came with so much responsibility.

After the original bliss of driving wore off, I felt overwhelmed by it all and loved it much less than expected. Maybe this was due to my early fumbling experiences; in spite of my general lack of maturity, I made it through that first year of driving.

I always loved the name of that first car and used to laugh to myself and make jokes about darting here and there.

Other cars came after because my dad loved to buy cars, so they changed almost as much as our homes.

That Dart, when I could use it, took me to school and to the store and to many local shops where I picked up things for mom or to the post office or to some cousins' home for a quick visit or to drop off or pick up some item (usually produce from a farm or the Eastern Market)for mom.

It took me around town.

That Dart also took me to the Parkview Cemetery and the parks where I could draw, walk, or delight in my freedom. I liked the occasional drive to anywhere and found some lovely places and walks there too.

One time, the Dart took me to the local Funeral Home. I had an assignment in my journalism class that was to interview a local business. In my quest for an atypical business,

I had an a-ha moment and thought it would be cool to interview a mortician.

That turned out badly.

I made the appointment, but when I got there, no one was around. I decided to investigate and walk through the hallways. Still no sign of any living person. Then I opened doors I shouldn't have opened. Behind one door was a dead body on the embalming table.

Horrified to the point of shock, I ran to the Dart, went home, and made up my interview. I had to turn it in the next day, so I wrote something that was entirely based on what I expected to happen instead of what really happened. I got a good grade but felt bad about the fiction; it actually was.

During my youth, I never learned anything much about fixing cars or changing tires. Truly, I was never interested in this. I followed my dad around for most of his other fix and repair projects but steered clear of car things.

To this day, I hate getting gas and try to time the need for gas for when John can get it for me. I am more than capable and have no idea why this aversion exists, but it does.

I've been thinking about getting an electric car for many reasons, and never stopping for gas is high on the list. In the end, I am fairly sure that I will hate pulling up to the electric charging station just as much as I hate getting gas. Walking is best, and I do that whenever possible.

I wonder what my dad would have thought of electric cars and cars without drivers. I can hear his laughter. Even though he may have thought this absurd at first, he would have investigated and learned about it and would have possibly come to a different conclusion.

He was always filled with wonder, so I am sure that

technology would have excited him, especially as it related to the car industry that he loved.

I often think about who in his young life in Ramallah was the one that he looked up to for inspiration and wonder. A brother, an uncle, his mother, a cousin? That is a question I wish I had asked him.

In the end, I love the gene that perfectly blends drive and wonder. The gene that brings so much adventure. It brings happiness from the satisfaction one gets from the daily practice of traveling from wonder and drive to experience and knowledge. I can see that same sense of drive and wonder in my children and grandchildren.

The mind that is filled with sense and wonder can dart here and there and take us on the best journeys of all.

My graduation day was from Bentley High School in Livonia, Michigan, June 1972.

VACATIONS

Vacations

The first big trip I took was a car ride to Niagara Falls with my entire family, except for my baby sister, Michelle. She was still little, and I think she stayed with my aunt Siham while we were away.

This trip was filled with excitement because my dad was always at the store, and we didn't get to spend extended periods of family time together very often. My father worked long hours every day in our grocery store, and mom was busy every day with her varied responsibilities of cooking, cleaning, and caring for her five daughters. That house on Terri Dr. always felt like a merry-go-round to me; one that never stopped, so the idea of spending several days and nights with the two of them in a new place was thrilling.

We went when I was around ten and Niagara Falls was a major destination in North America. One of the Seven Wonders of the World was right there in our upper backyard, so we were eager to head North. We lived in the southern part of Michigan near Detroit and were therefore able to drive to Niagara Falls. I think the drive was about four hours, but I remember it feeling so much longer than that.

The trip was memorable in so many ways, and I remember that first vacation with great fondness. The car was jam packed with two parents and four kids and all their gear and snacks. It was also filled with anticipation.

I can remember lots of bickering with four young girls in the car for what seemed like an eternity until we finally arrived at the great Niagara Falls. I remember being in the car and getting in trouble when we couldn't stop laughing or fighting or causing some sort of ruckus. I was a troublemaker when it came to any amount of uncontrollable laughter in the car. My dad would swing his arm back and tell us to stop right now, to settle down, to stop laughing. He would yell something in Arabic, and at times, he was seething with frustration which was fairly rare for him. My mom too, but that was more typical. We sisters really tried to keep it down, but after a few seconds, I would burst into laughter again, and the cycle would start over. Sharon was usually the second one to start laughing. If Michelle were in the car, it would have been her in second place or even first place, with me not far behind.

We stayed at what seemed to be a nice hotel, not that I knew any hotels at that point in my young life. Soon after we got there, we headed out and did a lot of walking all around the town.

I can remember the moment I saw the falls for the first time. I also remember looking at my father's face to witness his reaction. We had been talking about the falls before we went, and he told me what he thought they would look like. In the car on the way there, I remember wondering if the falls would be as he imagined. It's one of those places you never forget, like the Grand Canyon, or cathedrals in Europe, or the Northern California coastline and its giant redwoods, or the ocean when witnessed for the first time.

Memories of places are like icons embedded in my brain. I love to click on a memory and see the image I recall, usually with great clarity. Sometimes my senses become engaged, and I can recall the smells, taste the foods, and even feel some of the feelings I felt at the time.

Niagara Falls were just as amazing the second time I saw them, some 20 years later. I was awestruck in the same way when I witnessed my children seeing the falls for the first time. Like my father, I told them stories about the falls on the drive there, and they were filled with anticipation. When I was in Niagara Falls the first time, I had my first Chinese food. It was a mysterious, delicious experience and super fun all at the same time. Maybe you can imagine a big Palestinian family sitting down for their first Chinese meal, looking over the menu and trying to make sense of the dishes that were being offered. One thing that our cuisines had in common was the many, many dishes to share. We didn't know what we were ordering, but everything was delicious. We had everything from egg rolls to fortune cookies, and I've been in love with Chinese food ever since.

I was lucky to move to San Francisco in my teenage years and then enjoy the bounty of delicious Chinese food in Chinatown, which was superior to anything I ate in Niagara Falls.

I have always been a very adventurous eater, so I had no problem trying all of the beautiful dishes. Palestinian food is mostly about rice and lamb, and at times can look a bit monotone, but this Chinese food was filled with vibrant, shimmering vegetables, and that was aesthetically very pleasing to me.

After dinner, just as dusk approached, we walked around the falls and were thrilled to see all the sparkling lights shining on the falls and illuminating the mist in shades of lavender, blue, and rose. On one of the days that we were there, we went to see Lady and the Tramp at a great old theatre. We went to the matinee performance, and we were giggling with excitement. Going to a matinee was not something we did that often, let alone in a faraway place like Niagara Falls. I can remember the popcorn, the smell of that old, damp theater, and the joy and peace I felt with my family by my side.

I remember thinking, too, that little Michelle would have loved the movie and that I would tell her all about it when we got home.

As a young girl who was so excited about spending so much time with her parents, the truth is that I don't have many memories about my parents from that trip once we arrived at the falls. I have vivid memories of walking around town with them, looking at the falls in breathtaking awe with them, and the Chinese meal we all shared. I recall going to the movies with them that damp afternoon, and I still remember how it smelled like stinky old socks and shoes. Since then, every time I entered a bowling alley, the smell reminded me of that theatre.

All around the falls, there was so much to see, taste, and experience that I think my parents must have taken the back seat of my attention since I suddenly had so many new things to wonder about.

I don't have many distinct memories of the hotel room either, just that it felt so dark. I remember the car ride well, but once we arrived, a blur of excitement ensued. I can remember so much about the falls, the several rainbows we saw, and mostly that feeling of being awestruck at the marvel of it and the chilly and welcome mist on my face.

Another vacation from my younger years was when we went to Aruba. I was about seventeen at that time. This trip included an airplane and was a real vacation. Everywhere there were bathing suits, suntan lotion, fancy clothes for fancy dinners, big sun hats, and lovely sandals. Originally, I think the plan for that vacation was to go to Palestine, but with growing tensions, they had a Plan B. I always regret that we were never able to make that trip home with everyone.

Nonetheless, plan B filled us up with joy and excitement. My father and mother were so thrilled to be taking us on such a trip. Everything about that trip was perfect except for the fact that I managed to get a second-degree sunburn on the second day while eating mangoes by the pool and at the beach. It was worth it, though, as one of my very favorite memories was eating those mangoes on the beach with my dad. After buying a bag from a street vendor, we started eating. They were so tender you could bite straight through the skin, and within moments we were covered in mango juice. My dad and I loved to eat with reckless abandon. He was always a joy to eat with. To this day, I miss him when I am making something that I know he loves. I miss him just writing about these juicy mango moments in Aruba.

My dad loved to gamble, so it was no surprise that he picked a place with casinos. At times, he was a bit occupied with that, but the rest of the time we were all together and had a great holiday. We toured the town and all the vendor stalls; we saw the rock formation called goat bridge, which was magnificent. There were beautiful old churches and lots of goats everywhere. We ate so much seafood and some fruits and vegetables that I had never seen before. I loved being in the small town and talking with locals. It was fun buying our trinkets and trying all the delicious local foods. Mom loved Lladros, a Spanish brand of delicate porcelain figurines that she adored. In fact, most of our aunts did too. There was definitely a competition going on for who had the most or who had recently purchased a highly coveted piece. For some reason, unbeknownst to me, these Lladros became an obsession of sorts. Mom was collecting them as fast as she could, and she even bought a beautiful black and gold hand-painted curio cabinet just for them. Over the years, there was a lot of conversation about these Lladros, and which daughter would get which one, and even some fights. It's quite absurd in a way, but I think that we were all engaged because clearly these meant a great deal to my mom.

When in Aruba, I believe she bought two or three. One was of a young woman seated on the ground with a chicken and some pottery by her side. She gave that Lladro to me and said that the girl reminded her of me. I treasure the moment that she took to tell me that story more than the Lladro.

A couple of years before Aruba, I also got to go to Houston, Texas, to visit my uncle Badeah Mousa and my aunt Afaf Foteh. I was told that I could go there and help my aunt with her young daughter, Mona, who had been diagnosed with cancer. I remember sitting at Mona's bedside and reading to her. They had set up a bed for her on the main floor right next to the kitchen and family room. I would help with dishes, cooking, and helping Mona with her meals. I liked to just visit with her and watch some TV or listen to music.

This experience was so new to me, and even though I don't think I could fully comprehend what was looming in the future for Mona, her siblings, and her parents, I felt anxious and sad, and also relieved when I got out of the house. I remember thinking about my mom and dad and my sisters and how horrible it would be if something like this happened to our family…to any family.

This trip was also about spending some time with Dad's uncle, who lived in Houston. As a curious teenager, it was wonderful to learn more about my dad's relatives and their way of life in Houston. This uncle sponsored my dad's first trip to America and gave my dad so much opportunity and love.

My Uncle B, as we always called him, would drive around town running errands and checking in on his businesses. His driving was terrible; he would meander across lanes while tending to his pipe, lighting it, filling it to overflowing with his cherry tobacco. We were in a giant Cadillac, and it felt like I was cruising on a boat at sea instead of driving in a car on the road

After that, with white knuckles, I would arrive back at the house to see Aunt Olga, who was intense and extremely modern for her time. She was in full command of every detail of their existence. Lucky for me, she liked me a lot. My uncle loved to watch the old classic TV show "The Big Valley" every day while he had his lunch. I was certain that he really loved watching Barbara Stanwyck rule the roost in that big valley, and I'm certain that Barbara reminded him of his beloved Olga.

Another highlight was going to my uncle's clothing factory and getting to pick a few outfits. That factory was so large, and there were aisles and aisles of dresses. I remember so much polyester, which I came to detest, but at that time it seemed great, and all I could think of was the thousands of dresses and pant suits in every color and pattern imaginable. It was the late 60s, so one can imagine how wildly mod the prints were, and the colors were so bright. I remember picking a red and blue dress and also a yellow pantsuit. It was honestly overwhelming, and I don't think I wanted anything else.

I remember getting off the plane and seeing my father, who came to pick me up and was shocked when he saw me, because my body had changed that summer. Suddenly, I looked more like a woman than a girl. I remember that happening too and can recall being so self-conscious about it.

For the next many weeks, I was teased relentlessly by aunts and girls in my family. This was an unannounced and unwelcome event in my life. Suddenly, I was catapulted onto a stage and noticed by all the potential suitors in our community. Mostly, I was able to ignore the comments, and the suggestive leering looks of the young men because, quite frankly, I am quite sure I was unaware and quite naive at the time, but I do recall the strange discomfort I felt.

Eventually, before my next trip, which was our move to California, I did learn more about what it meant to be a young Arab woman (girl really) in a lineup of potential brides-to-be. But in those earlier days, I was dreaming of my times in Niagara Falls, Aruba, and Houston; I would say these were three unique trips for this young girl, and I always felt lucky to have had that odd collection of experiences.

WEEKENDS

Weekends

Large family gatherings made up most of our weekends. With wonderful food and family all around, it seemed everyone was so happy. Depending on the occasion or celebration (*haflah*), many times, aunts, cousins, and sometimes the uncles were all there. Cooking immense amounts of food and then savoring the dishes together was the best of pastimes.

Sometimes, some of the men even cooked, especially when they had a special dish they thought they were experts at. My father-in-law, Rizik Harb, loved to make his chicken liver dish for everyone. He started by sautéing the chicken livers in ample butter and olive oil, then adding tons of minced garlic, salt, and black pepper. After the livers were cooked, he would add chopped chili peppers and minced parsley. It was served with bread, and I for one loved it.

Other than these amazing family gatherings and feasts, our immediate family did not have any specific traditions for the weekends. Because my father worked in the grocery store most days, we didn't have the typical Saturday and Sunday time together as a family.

Since so many of our uncles also had stores, my aunts and cousins were in the same situation, so we spent many weekends together. The women would cook and gossip while the children played. The gossip was usually harmless and more of a cacophony of familiar Arabic voices, which I adored. I found these conversations to be melodic and quite comforting.

On a few wonderful Saturdays, Sundays, or some random day off during the week, we would take special trips to Belle Isle, Bob-Lo Island, or the Detroit Zoo. Bob-Lo was an incredible amusement park where you had to take a great old paddle boat to reach. I especially loved this excursion because the boat seemed so grand, and excitement filled the air. The lakes of Michigan were vast and beautiful and being on the lake in summer was idyllic. We would all run around the boat at will, stopping for an ice cream sandwich or a dance on the beautiful, shiny wood floor to the live band that played throughout the trip. I laugh when I think back on how our parents were apparently comfortable with us doing this. I'm not sure they even knew where we were. All too soon, we would arrive, dock, and proceed to get off. That was something in itself, watching the planks be set up and walking off the boat in a single file with great anticipation. Once on the island we would rush around trying to get on all the best rides and eat all the treats in between the rides. It was very typical amusement park revelry and the closest thing we ever got to Disneyland as children.

I am fairly sure that my dad's favorite trip was going to the Detroit Zoo, as we did this more often than any other outing. The zoo was always a great adventure, and I have many memories of dad showing us and teaching us about the different animals. He loved nature and animals in particular, and he was somewhat of an expert because, in most of his free time, he watched Wild Kingdom, the great animal show in the 60's and other nature shows that were popular in those days. And on many evenings, you could find him reading about animals in his encyclopedias. He used to say that he wanted to go to Africa on safari. I wish he had been able to do that. Maybe I will someday…

We would go to the Detroit Zoo often enough that we would see the same animals, "going to check on them," as he would say. He even had names for some of those animals.

Michigan, with all its beautiful lakes, afforded us many trips to the 'beach,' as we called it. I learned in California, many years later, about oceanfront beaches. But we sure loved the lakefronts and the pristine waters. As a child, I learned early that we would set up our blankets and our picnic a bit away from other beach goers, as we definitely did not represent the typical Michigan family.

We looked different, our food looked different too, and depending on which cousins we were with, and with mom and dad, our language was different as well. We kids spoke English mostly, but with newly immigrated cousins or aunts and uncles, the conversations were a mixture of Arabic and English. In fact, I found that most times, when non Arabs were close by, our families would start speaking Arabic exclusively. I don't recall that this bothered me so much until I was older but even then I found it interesting and wondered if they just didn't want others to know what we were saying? I spoke some Arabic and was enormously proud of our heritage and culture, so either language was okay by me.

On one beach trip to the lake, I remember dad telling us about being at the Dead Sea back home and how you could easily float because the salt content was so high. He was teaching me how to float when he told me that story. I loved his stories and mom's too, especially when they had to do with anything from their home country.

Another big part of our childhood weekends was when our huge and amazing family of aunts, uncles, and cousins would go on picnics. The best ones of all were the massive Ramallah community picnics. One in particular stands out and occurred when the Ramallah Convention happened in Detroit. All families from Ramallah could attend these conventions, and every year they held the convention in a different American city. These picnics were filled with our food, our music, our dance (*debke*), and the joy was contagious and unforgettable.

Growing up, I had this feeling of not needing any friends because I had so many cousins, and I am forever grateful for that endless bounty of love and support. The great tradition of gathering together and sharing meals had a way of sealing in the love. An endless stream of unconditional and familiar love.

My parents, who had arrived from Palestine several years prior, had been used to this tradition in their own country and carried it with them and held on to it tightly in America. I have always felt blessed and a part of something bigger. I have many memories of neighborhood children who were awestruck by all our gatherings and parties and would tell me that they felt envious. They would say something like, "There is always so much fun going on at your house."

And fun we had!

My father would host poker games (*shadeh*) on some Friday or Saturday nights. This was fun because I was fascinated by the gathering of the menfolk and the way they moved in the world. I would sneak downstairs while they were playing poker and take them something I knew they would like to eat or drink. I would stand around, watch, and listen. At some point, each of my uncles and my dad would 'sneak' me little bonuses like a dollar bill or sometimes a five-dollar bill. They would pat me on the head and tell me I was going to bring them good luck.

I'm fairly sure my sisters did the same thing, and I know for sure that my children Elise and Jameel did the same with their Sedo Shawky and their uncles when they stayed at Tata and Sedo's house overnight. I'm sure their cash take was much more than mine.

And now, throughout my adult life, and mostly on the weekends and of course the holidays, I plan as many family gatherings as I can. I believe this to be of the utmost importance to keep my tribe together. Our circle is a much smaller circle than the one I grew up with, but being together as often as possible and showering family with as much love and good food as I can is my way of life. When I think about weekends and what it might mean to some, it occurs to me that for my family from Palestine everyday was a 'weekend' where everyone was together and enjoying life as much as possible.

The Zoo tradition continues! This was in August 2017 at the Oakland Zoo with my granddaughters, Audriana and Amina.

NEIGHBORHOODS

Neighborhoods

By the time I was almost five years old, my dad had made lots of money in our store, and that allowed our family to move to a newly built home in the suburbs.

Before that, Detroit was our neighborhood. Towards the end of our time in Detroit and for a long time after, Detroit suffered. It had once been a thing of beauty, with the auto industry bringing in huge amounts of money and prestige. After decades of prosperity for some people and then their subsequent exodus to posh suburbs, Detroit became a shell of its former grandness. What followed was the rise of poverty and crime, and the city became a less desirable destination. The wealthy continued to move out, leaving behind avenues full of the ghosts of what once was. They left behind mansions with expansive, lush green lawns. Many of the homes, after sitting vacant for years, became a haven for the marginalized and homeless communities, allowing them a place to sleep and carry out their lives. Some parts of Detroit became overrun with crime and drug use. Some homes were burnt down. For so many, this was tragic to witness; to watch the decay unfold year after year.

The wealthy families of Detroit had moved out to places like Farmington Hills, Southfield, and Bloomfield Hills, to name a few, and left what was once beautiful Detroit behind. I don't think that they ever looked back. Attempts to regenerate Detroit continued, but the urban decay of the mid-20th century and rapid suburbanization was seismic and a constant topic of conversation while we were growing up there.

I love Detroit and always will. These days, the conversation is quite positive, and things continue as they have for many years now, to move in an upward and trendy direction. The restaurants, music, museums, architecture, Riverfront, and so much more make Detroit a wonderful destination. If you haven't been there, don't miss the Eastern Market, the Motown Museum, the DIA, the Fox Theatre, Pewabic Pottery, and the Arab American National Museum; a few of my favorites.

My parents and relatives would visit the Eastern Market often, as it was the destination for wonderful Arabic foods of all kinds. Once we moved out of Detroit, the city of Dearborn became the new spot, a town filled with Arabic stores, restaurants, and community. Many of the workers in the auto industry production lines were Arab, and when Ford moved its headquarters to Dearborn, many of the workers moved too. In recent years, Dearborn has become an Arab American majority city. The city is filled with so many wonderful restaurants and bakeries. As an adult, almost every time I took my children to Michigan to visit my parents and extended family, we would make a trip to Shatila Bakery and more recently to Masri for knafeh and other delights.

When my parents moved our family out to the idyllic rural outskirts of Detroit, I am fairly sure they thought it was a safer place to raise their children. I have many memories from my childhood of people talking about never going into Detroit, saying things like "you will only find trouble."

When I was young, there was much farmland in the rural area we moved to, and it truly did feel idyllic. We loved to go to the farms and pick fresh produce or just take drives in our beautiful cars when dad was off.

In this thrilling new landscape, I developed my love for watching the symmetry and beauty of the rows between the orchard trees as we sped down the road. I loved to sit in the back seat, mesmerized by the trick those trees and rows played on my eyes.

Often, we would drive to Big Boy's for hamburgers or the drive-through ice cream shop in Plymouth. These two spots were personal favorites and outings that lasted throughout the remainder of our time in Michigan.

I spent most of my childhood, from around age five to age 13, on a lovely little street called Terri Drive in Westland. This neighborhood made up my small world while growing up. I can remember so many details of this small subdivision, the tract pattern of its few streets, and the newly planted trees. I keenly remember the way it smelled in spring, the smell of the lawns and of the barbeques, and the sounds of the summer were thrilling. The memories of the falling leaves of autumn and the snowy perfection of winter, as we approached each Christmas, were Pure Michigan magic. The seasons of Michigan bring a cartful of memories to a child: blossoms and thunderstorms in spring, more storms and blooms, vegetables, and fruit in summer. Summer brought ice cream being made by hand using an old hand-cranked ice cream maker. In fall, apples, of course, and winter would bring more apples and pears, the smell of burning wood, and snow. Making angels in the snow was quite a scene with all the sisters lying on the snow and flapping their arms and legs to see who could make the best angel. Making snowmen was a fight to the finish to roll your snowball through virgin snow, and that was not easy with all of us running around in every direction. And small sloping hills were abundant, so sliding down the snowy slopes on old cardboard or the occasional sled was heaven-sent! Each of us trembling with cold and anticipation waiting for our turn.

I remember when we first moved to Terri Drive, some of the houses were not completed, and there were still many lots under construction. In fact, the house next door was still being built, and I remember playing teeter-totter on the large board that dad put over a barrel for us to play on. His ingenuity always amazed me.

At that time in Westland, it was still very rural and so beautiful. There continued to be a flood of folks moving out of Detroit and into the new suburbs. In truth, Detroit was only 30 minutes away, but in the late 50s and early 60s, crime and violence continued to increase, and we did not go to Detroit much at all. When we did go, it was to visit a relative for a holiday or such, and I always loved that because it always meant lots of cousins and lots of delicious food. I think we went to the Orthodox church once or twice during the early years of our times in the suburbs.

We had a lovely backyard that sat just above Edward Hines Drive. Below the drive was our beautiful park. We spent a lot of time in that park, a whole childhood in fact. In the early '60s, the world was a different place, and my mom would let us go to the park on our own. My father would come home from work and take us to the park. At some point, he would take his usual nap under the tree. He loved taking us to the park, and we certainly loved going there together.

So much so that it felt like a part of our backyard, as there was only a small gate that separated us. We would picnic there, play on the swings, roll down the hills, and go to the nature museum where Henry Ford built his first car. Once I captured a massive katydid and took it to that nature museum where they put it on a plaque under glass with my name on it, Patty Mousa... I was always so proud of that.

The katydid had fallen out of the tree just across the street from our house, and I found it there on the ground. It had already died, but it was so beautiful, and I remember running to the nature center holding it so carefully so that I did not damage its wings.

On the way to the nature center, there were trees of all sorts, but my favorites, those velvety red sumac, were on the right, so I always ran on that side of the road.

The houses in our neighborhood were mostly modest three-bedroom homes with a basement and wonderful yard space. There was one old house near the main road; the 'haunted house" as we called it that was surely inhabited by a family that farmed the land before the suburb was built.

We had a detached garage at the end of a long driveway. I can remember every detail of that house and all the changes that were made throughout our time there. My father planted a lovely garden behind our garage. I helped him plant that garden annually as often as I could.

The house was designed so all of us children could run from the living room through a small central hallway and through the bedrooms, then back through the kitchen into the living room. Yes, it drove my mom crazy, but it was the circular and dizzying rhythm of our childhood.

Even though the house seemed big when we moved in, in fact, it was quite small for four children, let alone five when my baby sister Michelle was born about three years later. My parents had one room; each of the other rooms was for two of the four girls. When Michelle came right before my eighth birthday, I don't remember where she slept after she was no longer in mom and dad's room.

My father soon created a room in the basement that was intended for Noel, as I recall, and maybe me to share. I don't remember sleeping there, though. I do remember his rustic shelving and other attempts at carpentry. Very rustic and yet quite functional.

One of my favorite aunts, Suad, her husband Rimon, who was my mother's brother, and their two children, along with my uncle Anwar also my mom's brother, moved onto our street when I was around nine years old. That was a most excellent time. We would play at their house often, and they would come to ours. I would walk by their house almost every day to wait for my dad to come home from the store. I would stop in for a snack because my aunt Suad was an amazing cook. We also passed their house while walking to school. It was nice to have a second home in the neighborhood. My poor Aunt Suad died in a terrible car accident picking up the cake for her daughter's birthday party while we were all at her house waiting for her to arrive. It was horrific beyond anything I think I experienced at that time, even beyond the death of my mom's mother in Ramallah, the Tata I never met.

I had a few playmates in that neighborhood. My favorite neighbor was Denise. After her, there were the twins Danny and Dale, and the Fehlners and the Millers. These neighbors were very friendly towards us and did not seem to mind our Palestinian traditions or I was too young to take any notice. One display of our traditions centered around the death of my Tata. This was when my mother's mother, Azizeh Dirbas, died. This happened just before my youngest sister, Michelle, was born, and it was a sad time in our home. My mom always dreamed of seeing her mom again, and that was never to be now. My Tata, the one I never met, died young, and I always imagined that if she were in America, she would have had better care and survived.

That day was a dark day on our idyllic Terri Drive. In the course of an hour, more than 20 cars came to our house. Everyone who came out of those cars was wearing black. Soon, they were all sitting in the house and in the backyard, the women inside and the men outside smoking. It felt as though there was a big black cloud over our home, with one car streaming in after the other, and people in black coming and going. I remember sitting on the front porch watching the black shoes and stockings streaming by me and noticing many of the neighbors standing out in their front yards or looking from their windows and porches. They didn't seem to mind, and curiosity was most of it. No one ever asked me about it, though.

I remember trying to get close to mom to see how she was and not being able to even get a glimpse of her on that terrible day. She was heartbroken, in shock, and unavailable to her daughters for some time. She had Michelle soon after, but the doctor had to induce her labor because my mother was already at or even past her due date when she got the news of her mother's death. Our new baby girl would just not come to us, as though this poor child knew that her momma was in trouble, and she should just stay put in the safety of her womb. When she finally arrived, we banded together; her four older sisters and we did the lion's share of caring for her. I remember changing her diapers, feeding her, and singing to her. Somehow, we all made it through that sad and difficult time. One time after changing an especially poopy diaper, I thought it would be a good idea to put a little perfume on her but dropped the bottle and some went in her mouth and up her nose! She started choking and I picked her up and quickly rinsed off her face and she seemed ok, but it took me quite a while to shake of the fear I felt when it happened.

There was a Catholic church, Saint Bernadine's, at the end of our street, and I was intrigued by how different this church was compared to the Orthodox church in Detroit that we sometimes attended. I used to go and sneak in on Sunday and stand in the back of the church and watch and wonder what these people were doing. Noel and I went to mass a few times and listening to the sermon was my least favorite part. I mostly enjoyed the songs and watching the families, the priests, the kneeling, and the standing. In the end, I couldn't wait to get to the creek.

Behind that church was a beautiful spring creek where my sisters and I would collect the pollywogs in jars, take them home, and watch them turn into frogs. I remember the anticipation of waking up every day to see how much they had grown.

Dad used to say in those early days that Terri Drive felt like the countryside compared to the inner-city spaces we had previously occupied. It was almost like farmland in those early days.

I had my first Bologna and American cheese sandwich on white bread with yellow mustard in that neighborhood, standing in front of our house with the kids from the block. It's been a favorite of mine ever since. Some of my fondest "American" food discoveries happened on Terri Drive. I remember being at another neighbor's, and they were eating spaghetti and meatballs. I told my mom about it, and she made our Arabic version with diced lamb meat and our red sauce over noodles, baked in the oven. At the end, she added caramelized onions and pine nuts! I'll take mom's version of spaghetti and meatballs any day.

One late afternoon, I saw my first cocktail hour at the Fehlners. Seeing Mr. & Mrs. Fehlner making martinis with a shaker was fascinating, and after toasting each other, they kissed, too! This was not something I had seen my parents ever do.

It was a common thing for me to go home and tell my parents about things I saw in some of the neighbors' homes, as they were so foreign to me. My dad wasn't so interested, but my mom sure was.

Mr. Miller across the street used to make his hand cranked strawberry ice cream and then take all of us kids around the block in the back of his truck while we ate the ice cream. No seat belts in those days.

My childhood was made up of the comings and goings in that neighborhood, and I have particularly good memories there. I remember getting on the rooftop with my dad during an ice storm and him taking movies of the view. To this day, I am shocked that he let me come up there with him. He would go up there to watch the forecasted tornadoes brewing. I remember one time when he scurried down and said he could see the tornado in the distance and gathered us all to the basement. Those storm days in the basement were so much fun. No tornado ever hit our home. Many years later, I asked him about those times and asked why he let me follow him up there. He turned and said, "you followed me everywhere, and a roof was no different" and I am fairly sure that I was stubbornly going to do it, even if he said no.

I remember when the streets flooded during a big storm, and all the kids in the neighborhood were frolicking in the streets of water up to our knees. I wonder how foul that water probably was, but as per usual, kids always survive the crazy things they do when they're small. I did, and I know I am probably better for it.

When I wasn't hanging around on Terri Drive, I would be at school and sometimes at the store or at a cousins house.

Growing up in our grocery stores in some ways was like being in a small neighborhood with our regular customers coming in daily.

I learned about all kinds of foods while living in and around the Detroit area.

As time unfolded in our homes and in our stores, I loved learning about the ingredients for the two food pillars in my life: Palestinian and American food.

I can't remember a time when I wasn't eager for a meal to be served, no matter where I was. The Palestinian dishes I grew up with are wildly delicious, and I felt ravenous when they were about to be served because I knew how good they would be.

The anticipation started when we would go to the Arabic food stores in Detroit and Dearborn. Usually, this trip included an aunt or two and a big cart of all our favorites. Every aisle had something I yearned for, the mixed nuts and seeds we would all sit around and eat in the evening. The majesty of all the various herbs for our mom's tea *(shai)*, mom's specific blend was perfect. The fruits, vegetables, fresh cheeses, labna, and yogurt were so beautiful.

This bounty of goods could not be found in our neighborhood markets, nor in our own store. I am certain that having my food experiences so close to Detroit, where access to all the foods of my people gave me a keen appreciation and backdrop from which to grow my love for our food.

I loved those trips to Dearborn and the Eastern Market and would always be eager for the next market day and our favorite neighborhoods. The sights, the smells, and the sounds of our native language and sometimes our music were hugely satisfying.

After shopping, we would head home to our neighborhood, and we would cook, and then we would happily all eat together. Later we would have shai and fruit or some other sweet treat that we may have brought home from Dearborn.

As a child, my family moved many times. Terri Drive was our first stop in the suburbs, and many homes came after that.

That first home in the suburbs was not diverse, which as I got older, I grew to sense a sometimes awkward veil over our Arab presence. Most families were nice, and we played with most of the kids in the neighborhood, but our parents did not really participate beyond their friendly hellos. They did not mix much, if at all, with the neighbors, so that left us mostly on our own with the neighbors and their kids.

There was a wonderfully kind Chaldean family up the street, and after a couple of years, one of my aunts and uncles moved into a house on Terri Drive, along with two other Ramallah families. We had our own little Palestinian family right there on that street.

When I became a teenager we started moving as though we were on the run to somewhere. Looking back, I believe my father was restless and ultimately wanted to move to California, where several of his siblings lived. My mom also loved to move to a nicer, bigger house and she could be very persuasive too. In the end, as a couple they were aligned in this regard.

We moved from Terri Drive to Ellen Drive just off of Five Mile Road, and then to our biggest Michigan home on Six Mile Road.

Ellen Drive was a new bi-level home in a fancy new neighborhood. My mother was thrilled to be in what was our community considered a fancy neighborhood. When I returned so many years later, it was still quite a special place and impeccably clean, with manicured homes and fancy cars in the driveways. The creek and turkey farm still rambled through the pastures behind our home. All the trees were now massive and luxurious with their shade and various hues of green.

On the other side of the neighborhood was a beautiful golf course.

We were surrounded by every color of vegetation in summer with vast blue skies overhead that boasted the most voluminous clouds and in those days, plenty of snow in the winter. The four seasons of Michigan were filled with their own particular beauty. This few year stop on Ellen Drive was especially lovely as this was the neighborhood where I met my first best friend, Karen, drove my first car; that pale yellow Dodge Dart, and had my first crush on the boy across street.

Time gets swept away but some things remain and color the pages of one's life. Karen and I are still friends, I dinged and battered that car, and that boy never noticed me. The moment that I take with me of that first sweet crush was the day Jimi Hendrix died, and we sat on the front lawn together and I consoled him while he cried. He loved music and his new red Mustang, but alas, never noticed me at all.

This home on Ellen Drive was all about transition for me. So much was happening, and it was all happening too fast. Time and events flew by like snowflakes; wild, wonderful, gone in a second, and impossible to hold onto. Before we knew it, we were packing again moving up the road to a big house on Six Mile Road. We had fun times in that house and an incredible New Year's Eve party that was as much fun planning as it was at party time. I remember eating so much American style party junk food that was included in our vast menu that soon I got the worst tummy ache, and midnight was welcomed with a cup of mom's *shai.*

The acceleration of our lives was going into warp speed. In the end, my first childhood home on Terri Drive was filled with wonder, allowing me to explore the great outdoors whenever I wanted. The other homes brought their own abundance and experiences there on those streets with my sisters and mom and dad; all of which I hold close and treasure.

A home is what you make it, and growing up in Michigan was lovely as it allowed me to absorb the beauty of nature through the seasons, leaving an indelible mark on my spirit. There was as much space as a child needed on this streets in those green spaces to take in the universe.

They say moving is hard on kids, but I believe moving allows for deeper exploration and experience. While it's true that familiarity, tradition, and consistency are important foundations for children, there are treasures to be found everywhere if you keep your eyes wide open.

Adapting is definitely one of my strengths. I think this came from being a first-generation Palestinian American and moving as much as we did. The constant moves along with the steady in-flow of relatives with their endless new stories and love facilitated my resilience and ease in the world.

I only have the experience that I had and can't say what it would've been like to stay in one home my whole childhood. My childhood was filled with a treasure trove of vivid memories of so many adventures, of my sisters, of the outdoors, of the homes we lived in, and of my parents... those two...always on the move.

My beautiful parents, Shawky & Jannette, on the move.

MORNING

Morning

It seems to me that most people are either morning or evening people.

Throughout my life, I have been unwavering in my love for morning time. I am a morning person through and through who loves to be awake and witness the gift of dawn. On most mornings, even cold mornings, I stand at the open door or step outside into the garden to watch and listen. The sounds and the smells of the morning are lovely. These moments remind me that all is well in my little corner of the world. They fill my soul and lift my spirit to a place that fuels my day. With every breath of morning air, I find peace and serenity in the quiet morning sounds of nature. I find it cleansing and uplifting to stand at the edge of a morning like this.

I love getting up in the predawn hours with great anticipation for the day. I especially enjoy the quiet and watching the sunrise. In my 20s, I started to drink coffee, and that has become a most beloved component of my morning ritual.

The way I then navigate through my day is quite simple. As far back as I can remember, I've been a fireball in the morning. That ball of fire burns bright throughout the morning, starting to burn out as the late afternoon and evening approach. As a child, I remember feeling sleepy after dinner and would welcome bedtime most nights. I felt confused when some of my sisters, mostly Sharon and Michelle, would get wound up as bedtime was upon us.

My energy starts to wane around three o'clock almost precisely every day. I wake between four and five most days, so my energy reserve is determined by that. I still have energy left in the afternoon, but I don't like to do any kind of work that requires much critical thinking after two or three. Around that time is when my more creative side emerges, and I like to save these creative impulses for the afternoons and evenings. The morning is more cerebral for me, and in fact, I have written these stories mostly in the predawn hours.

Each day is a gift that I cherish and I do my best to share my appreciation for the new day with the universe. I have never used an alarm clock because my internal clock wakes me up almost to the minute after seven hours of sleep. My family, friends, and colleagues all know that I am an early person. Those who are also morning people understand this morning community and respect each other's quiet morning moments, for the most part.

It's funny because many of the people in my life are evening people, and I don't mind that at all, because my creative evening self takes pleasure in their company and spirit.

Morning person, evening person … you are either one or the other, and it's not something you can fight, nor should you. My dad always used to say, "If your hair wants to part on the right, don't try to part it on the left." I agree wholeheartedly and love all the morning times he and I had together. Growing up, he was my morning comrade.

Even my favorite beverage is the morning coffee. I love my morning coffee, and there is no rival for the feeling or the anticipation I feel while making it. As I got older, there's the ritual to love, and for me, it takes place in that dreamy pre-dawn part of the day that I covet. Just me and my coffee in the dim light.

In fact, I often go to sleep thinking about waking up and

having my coffee. This is an emotional response that's about much more than the actual beverage. It has to do with gratitude and the possibilities and beauty of each new day, and certainly the intensely beautiful memories of my childhood and the morning ritual of coffee.

Memories of the cardamom scented *kahwa Arabia* while making my father his favorite coffee are a constant companion. These are delightful memories to reminisce about with my sisters, as he used to tell each of his five daughters that they made the best coffee. What a great trick! He always got a great cup of coffee, and we were each encouraged to please him because of his constant praise.

This *kahwa Arabia* was a heady and aromatic brew with cardamom pods and sugar added to the finely ground dark roast coffee and made in a tallish narrow-necked brass or aluminum *(ibrik)* pot. The handle was quite long because it would get hot while you held the pot and watched the coffee brew and foam up to the top. When the foam was building, you would remove it from the flame, let it settle down, and then return to the flame to foam up again. This method was repeated three times. At the end, a few drops of water were dripped over the foam, and the pot was covered with a small saucer for a moment before serving.

After the coffee was enjoyed, sometimes we would turn our little demi cups over on the saucer and let the residue drip down the sides for a fortune reading of the cups. Yes, this is actually an art for some true fortune tellers, but mostly we just made up stories of good fortune or wishes.

My parents had coffee every morning and usually throughout the day; always, a fresh pot of American coffee presided over the kitchen counter. It would be unheard of not to have fresh coffee waiting for whichever relative stopped by. Coffee, sometimes American and sometimes Arabic, was always included in the lively discussion between my mom and her many siblings. Something else to argue about, like which store had the best price for coffee, the brands, the size, and the roast type. They did this weekly about coffee, lamb meat, produce, and Tide, Cascade and toilet paper came up often.

All these exciting conversations happened over coffee, which certainly encouraged a livelier banter. I will always cherish those moments of them carrying on as they did, while my father would usually sit silently by and just enjoy his coffee.

After my dad was mostly retired, I remember many a morning when, upon waking, I would listen for sounds, and usually those sounds came from the kitchen. Most times I would find my dad already drinking kahwah and my mom already in a cooking trance. I learned about that trance and can fully appreciate the singular and undeniable joy it brings. Momma started her cooking early, especially when we were having company. Dad was close by, sitting in his pajama bottoms and T-shirt. He himself was also in a trance of sorts as he was in heaven when mom was cooking early. He could anticipate all the delicious dishes that were coming his way.

I remember one of these mornings when he spoke again of mom's first dinner she made for him after they were married. Those stories fed my soul and taught it to love the gifts that come in the morning.

My other favorite beverage is tea. I am equally passionate about tea, but in a different way, without as much anticipation and buildup as with the morning coffee experience. Tea comes with a different set of emotions and memories that have to do with the calm of late afternoons or evenings, which were times for family relaxing and visiting.

In our home, we drank *shai*, a beautifully brewed tea made with mint, chamomile, sage, and anise. The aromas are exquisite, and it is the most comforting and nurturing tea in my experience.

Growing up, having a cup of *shai* meant you were really taking care of yourself—whether you had a tummy ache, weren't feeling well, or it was really cold outside, or some other moment that required a time out.

Pretty much everyone in our family has tea every evening and coffee every morning. My children do the same in their own families, and I know they share this sentiment. The warm beverage to start the day and the warm beverage to end it; a lovely cup to begin the day and a lovely cup to dream sweet.

FOOD

Food

I can't remember a time in my life when I was not in love with all the foods there are to eat in the world. It's vast; it's miraculous, really, and I have always felt so lucky to live in a family that adored food and, most importantly, respected the tradition of preparing honored dishes for family.

When I wasn't at school or in our store, I was at home with my mother and often my aunts, or at their homes, learning about and cooking Palestinian food. My mother's food always took first place, and I paid close attention to what she did and to whom she looked up to and learned from.

Subsequently, the two aunts I learned the most from were Azizieh and Suad. Along with mom, they were the holy trinity of the most delectable dishes. Together, they instilled in me a wild desire to try everything and taught me that in order to deliver the ethereal tastes of our dishes, it was necessary to be intense and joyful in the kitchen. This joyful state of mind was required at the market or on the farms while planning the meals as well.

The joy seed for food was tossed around by my father too and the seeds grew in our family and thrived there throughout our lives. He loved food his entire life and it was always a joy to eat anything with him. I know mom loved to cook for him as he was so excited about every meal. His love of food helped to fuel her passion to learn and then to perfect every dish.

Hot summer nights in Michigan were always a reason to crack open a big, juicy watermelon. Dad teased me that the "watermelon seed" birthmark on my right thigh was proof of how much watermelon he, my mom, and all my ancestors had eaten. I love that I carry this watermelon seed mark. It reminds me of where I came from.

My daughter Elise has the same birthmark, and we all love watermelon especially when served with some nice cheese and bread.

Growing up, my favorite foods were always the Palestinian dishes, without exception.

The aromas of the kitchen, the sounds of chopping, and the chatter or sometimes singing during the preparation were like a clarion call. The shared anticipation filled the room with a perpetual good mood. This spirited experience surrounding the preparation of our traditional dishes is as old as Palestine and transcends generations.

We excitedly gathered around the table to enjoy each dish. We savored the flavors and commented on how tender the lamb was, or how fresh the *kusa* was, or how sweet the green beans were. We paid attention to how things tasted and had profound respect for the cook and their offerings. We weren't just eating, we were experiencing the food and filling our bellies and souls with the flavors of our ancestral home.

My children and grandchildren look so forward to every Palestinian dish I prepare, whether it be a small plate of cheese, olives, and tomatoes or the feast of *Maqluba.* This Palestinian word means 'flipped over' because this heavenly rice, lamb, and vegetable dish is layered in a large pot, and when complete, the family gathers around to see the pot flipped over onto the serving tray. We make ours with cauliflower, chickpeas and sometimes eggplant.

These shared experiences all came to us with the indelible

handprints of our ancestors and all the dishes they made with those hands for their families from the beginning of time.

The preparations usually included a story and maybe even a song about the dish. All part of the experience, this contributed to our healthy appetites. Like many families with a strong food heritage, the children would line up in anticipation of the delicious dishes their families prepared. It was celebratory and usually involved many family members in the making of the dishes.

Some of the dishes were quite exotic, like the stuffed lamb intestines and roasted lamb brains with garlic and parsley. Lamb spleen pockets stuffed with onions and lamb, hand-sewn to close and then roast. *Kibbeh Niyeh,* a minced raw lamb mixed with the finest of bulgur wheat and spices, is a family favorite. In the old country, they did not waste any part of the animal, and I have a deep appreciation and respect for that. This philosophy carried over into my first-generation life from growing up in Michigan to the rest of my life in California. As a child, I ate from all of these dishes and found them delicious. My dad even offered me a $ 5.00 bill if I ate the eyeball of a lamb, when they had roasted the lamb's head and served it in a yogurt soup. I did, and it was good, although I think I just swallowed it whole. That's the only time I remember that dish being made. Over the years, some of the more 'exotic' pieces of the animal went by the wayside as butchers didn't cut from the whole animal any longer, so the internal organs and byproducts of the animal were not as readily available.

Some of my other favorite dishes are *Molokiah, Shish Barak,* and always *Hashwa.* They are only my favorites by a little because I love most of our dishes equally. I can honestly say that I do not remember any Palestinian dish that I didn't find superb. It is about the fragrance and the uniquely supreme flavor.

The beloved Tabbouleh is divine, and that dish came with the Tabbouleh song when I was young. I especially remember my Aunt Najla, who loved to sing while cooking. There are many variations of this magnificent salad, but I love ours the best. Hand-minced parsley, delicious fresh-squeezed lemon juice, and bright green fresh olive oil from Palestine whenever possible. The season's best tomatoes and fine bulgur. We like to eat it with the hearts of romaine using the smallest leaves to scoop up a big bite of the treasured salad.

The pleasure from the intense experiences I had around these dishes and the activities associated with them is in large part why they are the most cherished and eclipsed many other foods. I know that anyone reading this who has a favorite meal from their childhood, especially one marinated in heritage and cooked with ancestral spirit, will agree.

There is something about the sensory experience that sticks with you. Enjoying a meal layered in experience and seasoned with joy is the most comforting thing of all, a comfort that can't be replicated.

There were many celebrations in our lives, and a Palestinian celebration is always built around the required feast. One of my favorites is when our family moved to California. Our first stop was at my uncle *(amo)* Fuad and aunt (*amti)* Nuha's home in Daly City. After the heady *mezzeh* start of the meal, large platters of *Musakhan,* chicken roasted with sumac, onions, and pine nuts served on pita bread, leg of lamb, and fragrant pine nut and almond-topped rice were served. Fresh-baked pocket bread, yogurt, stewed vegetables, and stuffed grape leaves, our adored *warak dawali* An endless rhythm of food and joy. Truly, one must witness to believe. This was miraculous to me, like the 8th wonder of our world which I embraced fully and knew would remain a centerpiece of my life forever. I was in love with all of it felt so grateful to the Gods for my heritage and to the knowledge and keen awareness that I was part of something ancient and magnificent.

When I think of that day, it still represents an outpouring of love, of heart and soul, and everything that we do for family by way of celebration through the bounty and the beauty of food. To partake in this beautiful expression of love is a calling of sorts, a force and deep desire for continuity and connection to heritage.

And then there is the infiltration of all the other foods that I learned to love. Slowly over time, lots of "American" dishes were making their way into my repertoire. Growing up in a grocery store created an opportunity to try new things, especially junk food, processed, and otherwise unseemly goods. But it also gave way to ongoing and seasonal exposure to produce and seasonal items.

As I grew older, I was able to identify the good stuff, and many incredible dishes seeped into my life and indeed found their way to my heart. I was lucky to travel so much, and I loved dining at restaurants. In fact, for many years going to restaurants was absolutely my favorite pastime. I loved the food sections of the papers and devoured Saveur, Gourmet, Edible Art, Food & Wine, Bon Appétit, Slow Food, and anything else I came across. The 70's and the 80's were an exciting time for the food scene. California and Nouvelle Cuisines were pivotal and transformative, and I was an eager audience. I was in my 20s and 30s and filled with desire for every new food experience. My children and the food scene were my everything.

So, in this intoxicating period, I grew to love so many new dishes, things I had never experienced like fresh oysters, arugulas and other mind-bending greens and radishes, bisques and soups of all kinds, paella, shrimp, tacos, sushi, clam garlic and pesto pizza, pasta Bolognese, a perfectly roasted chicken and divine artisan breads with butter and sea salt at the Zuni Café on Market. I could list so many restaurants right now and tell you in detail about my favorite dish on their menu, but I will do that on another day in another book.

This period changed me forever, and yet even with the new foods I lusted after, I never lost my first love for the food of my people.

Anticipating our dishes came with the ultimate desire; a food state of mind that I shared with dad and also my youngest sister, Michelle. Don't get me wrong, I'm sure all my other sisters loved to eat as well, but I am referring to that certain and wild "I'll rip your head off if you get in the way of what I am about to eat " lust for food. If you are like this, you know who you are. There is an actual Arabic saying that my Aunt Azizieh (who shared this lust) used to say that in Arabic translates into something like this: God help the person who gets between me and my food!

My dad's passion for food was also witnessed while he was cooking and preparing things for the store's meat case. I loved watching my dad create interesting ready-to-roast products in the butcher department, and also later on sandwiches and such in the deli. He was a lover of food and got excited about setting his service cases and making a great sandwich, or the city chicken, or tying the roasts. And he loved to paint signs for all of his daily specials. He had excellent penmanship that I literally copied and mastered as I watched him make these signs. He was proud of these signs and of his excellent command of his writing in English. His enthusiasm for his products showed in those wonderful handwritten signs.

Dad took immense pride in his butcher trade, which was mostly self-taught. He learned quite a bit from a special person at one of our stores in Plymouth, Michigan. His name was Mr. Unger, a wonderfully kind and quiet German man who, like my father, emigrated to America in search of a more sustaining and satisfying life. Mr. Unger would give my sister Noel and me a fresh bottle of chocolate milk when he saw us. I still remember his smile. He taught my Dad many butchering tips, and they seemed to have a good friendship, but I never heard of him again after we left that store in Plymouth. One thing I remember with fondness is how he taught my dad, who later taught me to tie the meat roasts. My daughter also knows how to tie roasts like that now and I'm sure she will show her children too.

It was fun to be with dad when he was doing anything with food. I learned so much about making do, adapting recipes, selling food, and engaging the customers in that Meadowdale Market neighborhood. I learned to be resourceful, not waste and to be as efficient as possible. I watched as Dad always gave 110%. He was never afraid to try things, and many times he would hastily do a job, and the outcome may not have lasted long, but he was incredibly creative with a great imagination. If he saw a problem, he wanted to fix it. He did the same with foods he was long on, always a solution to use them up before they went bad, or he would just bring them home. That man could save anything! Many times, he would make a delicious stew at the store that we and the employees would all enjoy together.

I feel proud of the food knowledge I have accumulated in my 70 years. Honing my singular experience with every food that I have ever cooked or eaten. The meals I have shared and the experiences surrounding them are endless. I hope this life brings me more lovely repasts that nurture the soul, and if I die tomorrow, I will have been blessed with more delicious food than one could ever dream of.

Sometimes I wonder about the possibility of a person knowing which meal precisely was the best they had ever had. I find this to be an impossible question.

Because of my love for food and my career in food, I am asked this question often. I understand why someone would ask this of me, as I have been living, working in, and loving my life with food for decades.

My love of food transcends much in my life, and I believe that most meals are incredibly special, so how on Earth could I pick one meal? Being in the food business allowed me extensive travel, and during these trips, I have had access to the most amazing foods and meals, often in people's homes on land that their families have owned for generations.

My passion for what I came to know of gastronomy expanded with each new food adventure. Standing side by side with producers and helping create their particular product gives an insight that can't be measured. These moments informed my palate and my knowledge with vast contributions to the food library that lives inside of me. I felt great humility as I watched and learned and felt it was an honor and also a responsibility to pay it forward and share what I could.

Whether it is the beautiful blue cheese made in the

Piedmont region of Italy in Castelmagno at an altitude of almost 4,000 feet or Culatello from Rome, or a classic paella from Barcelona, pulpo made moments after it was plucked from the sea of Crete, or the simplicity of a luscious handful of blueberries from Michigan shores, any dish made from cherished food becomes something sublime.

Food has never been just a meal to me; it is the sum of so much more.

Just *when* and *where* does a person become aware of their passion for gastronomy, though? For me, the answer is easy. As a child, watching my mom and aunts doing their thing in the fields and in the kitchens, I was sitting on the edge of my seat and ready for more. This feeling was further solidified watching my dad in the kitchen or our store doing his thing, too. Food was all around all the time and what's not to love? Eating is one of life's most intoxicating pleasures, and when food is prepared with intention and so much love, it communicates to our bellies, but our emotions and senses lustfully awaken too. I had the good fortune of being raised with so much food culture and tradition, and this took on a life of its own.

I know that for me, the love of gastronomy (the art of choosing, cooking, and eating good food with friends and family) landed in the deepest part of my belly, which is where I believe my emotional spirit and imagination live. It is woven into the fiber of my whole self, it seems. I think about food every day, what I need to use up first, buy, or pick from the garden, and what I will make. It is a beloved pastime that I have shared with everyone I care about. It is like a beating organ, which is neither stomach nor heart, nor mind; it has its own place, a place that informs my day.

So, for me it is indeed impossible to think of the best meal.

This question reminds me of Mozart, when he was asked to take out some notes in his new composition. He wondered, Which notes should I remove? What a ridiculous question, he thought that removing notes, or even one single note would change everything entirely.

Meals are like a complete history for me, a composition, and a journey; I can't pick one over another. It is just impossible as they are all embroidered together to create my beautiful epicurean canvas of recipes and food moments. They all mean something to me.

I don't follow recipes that frequently, as I like to use what I have on hand, and I love to cook with all of my senses. What does this mean? It means that I like to look at what's beautiful and seasonal, I'd like to listen for hints of what family and guests want to eat, I like to smell the spices in the ingredients as I'm putting them in, and often my decision is changed based on how it smells in the moment. And, of course, tasting, tasting, tasting.

When it comes to Palestinian dishes, however, I follow recipes with precision, and these honored recipes do not deviate in any way, shape, or form. These are sacred to me, and my favorite Arabic dishes are numerous. I don't think I can pick a favorite, like my aunt Azizeh used to say, "The meal in front of me is my favorite!" I can honestly say that is how I see it as well.

I do have some dishes that I especially covet. Those are *Shish Barak,* little lamb, and pinenut filled tortellini like pastas floating in an incredible soup made with yogurt, mint, and garlic. Another favorite is *Imnazzalah,* a dish of eggplant, pine nuts, small pieces of leg of lamb, onions, and tomatoes served over rice pilaf. And *Hashwah*! This is that heaven-sent rice dish filled with lamb, pine nuts, onions, and allspice.

It's easy for one to see what our main ingredients are in the Palestinian pantry.

Converted Rice for Mahsi
Long Grain Rice for everything else
Lamb
Yogurt
Jars of Grape Leaves (Fresh whenever you can get them)
Pinenuts
Bulgur wheat
Tahini
Sumac
Chicken
Zaatar
Allspice
Chickpeas
Olives
Olive Oil
Dried Molokiah
Khubiz

Fruits and vegetables are in abundance, and when we can pick fresh grape leaves, we do, and if the market has fresh Molokiah, we buy it and pick it.

The only thing I like more than food is the cooking of the meal, and the preparing of the table, and at the top of the list is the gathering and enjoyment of the meal and each other's company.

I feel truly blessed to say that I have never been hungry and that the foods I grew up with were so nutritious, allowing me, my sisters, and my family to thrive. It's not just that the food was available; it was delicious and healthy, too. I say this with the deepest gratitude because I know that this is not everyone's experience.

I have spent much of my career as a food buyer and receive many samples, which I love to share with pretty much anyone I come in contact with. I take chocolate bars to my hairdresser, cheeses to my doctors, delicious cookies and cakes to my gardeners, and all manner of foods to my family, neighbors, and colleagues. The list is endless, and I think anyone who knows me has probably been the recipient of these shared goods and has given feedback on everything they got to try.

But none of these new foods could ever compare to the Palestinian dishes that have nurtured my life in so many ways. It is with immense pride and joy that I believe these cherished dishes will continue to be the favorites of my children and grandchildren, and as it goes, I can certainly hope that my great-grandchildren will know at least a few of the foods from their Tayta Patricia.

Food is the manna that binds generations; it's the icing on the cake, the cream in your coffee, the cherry on top.

Better yet, it is the hummus on your bread (*khubz*)

Continuing traditions of harvesting the bounty! Audriana and Amina making Plum Jam in Walnut Creek in July 2019

Momma and her beautiful Olives.

Warak Dawali and some of my Palestinian Pottery. These grape leaves were hand-picked from the ridge above our home in Walnut Creek. We always have some grapes too. They are tiny but so delicious.

And to my daughter, Elise: Mamool, for her wedding day! These are made with a kalab, the wooden mold that makes the domed Mamool (or these date filled 'wreaths', formed by hand). The little pincher tool in the photo is used to "pinch" the dough and create the beautiful patterns.

CHANGE

Change

It is not easy for people to change, but I know it's possible. I know this from my own personal experience. Over the years, I have witnessed changes in myself. Some changes may be small while others hold more magnitude, but they all matter, especially when they are changes for the better, changes that improve my relationships and experiences.

Each of us is born into a circumstance. If we are lucky, we are born to two loving parents and an extended family. In a scenario such as this, we are submerged into a collection of ideals and behaviors that can be both loving and supportive. Day by day and year by year, we use every sense to absorb what we hear, see, feel, smell, and taste. If you think about it, it's like an avalanche of inbound information and experiences that will shape much of who we become.

These sensory experiences are some of the ingredients that create identity. Of course, genetics plays a factor as well, but I believe our life experiences make up much of who we are. Life experiences can also be the vehicles that open pathways to change.

Being a first-generation child starting school had its own unique experiences. As this child makes the transition into a foreign world that is much bigger than what came before, they start accumulating more experiences that are completely new and sometimes foreign to them. Suddenly, their little lives are filled with many new sights and sounds. They learn about new foods; they hear different kinds of music and different conversations. They observe a multitude of activities that they have not previously witnessed. This is true for most children but is especially true when the child's ethnicity and home culture conflict with the traditional American school culture.

Other kids' homes are set up differently from theirs, and because family dynamics are unique to each family, the aesthetic, and the personalities of the new humans they interact with at school are not what they have experienced in their own homes. These many new moments of life are merged with what they know so far, and thus, their personality continues to develop based on these new experiences. The fabric of who we are continues to develop and mature through the balance of our lives, thread by thread, layer by layer. Along this journey is where change happens.

For me, the biggest change in myself happened when I met a man who later became my life partner. His name is John, and it is easy for me to recall every detail of the day I met him. Looking back, I believe that what I experienced that day was a profound unconscious awareness that this person would change my life forever. From that first moment, John treated me differently, and I loved being around him. I recognized that I felt different when I was with him; I felt respect and equality. Up to that point in my life, I hadn't truly felt this kind of unconditional acceptance. He was straightforward, honest, and kind. He had a serious side but also a lighthearted way about him. He just made me feel seen.

For reasons not yet fully understood in my early life and as I moved into my 20s, I had the notion that I was less important and held less power than the men in my world. Even so, I had a pretty dynamic personality, was stubborn at times, and even defensive when I felt I had to stick up for myself. With all this, I felt insecurities that at times caused me confusion, which sometimes affected my decisions. In fact, I'm not sure that I really made that many decisions along the way, as I believed I was supposed to just do as I was told, especially in my early life or ....I just went with the flow with broad strokes of impulsiveness.

By the time I met John, I was in my early 40s and twice divorced with much life under my hat. I had been through complex situations that were, at times, very disappointing and almost catastrophic. I found my way through those times and to a new place of peace and a different sense of self.

In my 30s, I got divorced from Jerry, the father of our children, and this was the first divorce in our family. My parents were extremely disappointed. My dad never said much, but I could see the disappointment and confusion (maybe anger) in his eyes. My mother was beyond embarrassed (I know this because she told me many times) and hotly cruel, and I felt cast off by her. She continued to help with the kids but treated me with disdain as 'I had caused her so much shame in our community.' She called me all kinds of names and yelled at me nonstop. She told me not to come to her house. I knew she was angry and sad and that she did not really mean all the things she was saying. I felt empathy for what she was going through, all because of me. It wasn't long before she let go of her anger and most of her resentment, even when I went full throttle into doing whatever I wanted to do. After this horrible divorce period of our lives, I let the pendulum swing much too far in the other direction.

I believe that time in my life is when I belatedly experienced my adolescence, willfulness, and rebelliousness. During this wild period of my life is when I met wild and eccentric Paul, who would become my second husband.

When Paul and I met, my first divorce wasn't yet final, and during this time, he came to the rescue to support me and my children. He always seemed to be around. I fell for his engaging and charming ways. At first, I had no interest in him romantically, and then, as best as I can understand it, I saw his never-ending support as true love and dedication to me and to Elise and Jameel. Later I learned of his very intentional motive to marry me.

The first few years of our life together were filled with adventure and fun times. His devotion to the kids and to their education was steadfast, and things were always moving so fast with him that time marched on at a head-spinning pace. He was a whirlwind every day, and I chalked it up to his being eccentric. After a few years and what I thought was a misplaced letter from his doctor, which I later found was intentionally placed for me to see, I learned that he was bipolar and also suffered from "illusions of grandeur," as the diagnosis read. His behavior was manic and so was his spending.

This hit me hard, and I knew it was all true, as we were already struggling financially, and I knew he was spending money without my knowledge. At that time, I did not understand how much betrayal and deceit were occurring as I naively wanted to trust him, and that was my biggest mistake. The idea of a second divorce made me feel ill, so I marched on.

Looking back, as I learned more, it's easy to see that he was not well and would not take his medication for his bipolar illness. This was a recipe for disaster, and that is exactly what unfolded.

We had a crazy and impulsive short experience in Michigan that ended in bankruptcy. He convinced me that we should move cross-country, from California to Michigan. My parents had recently moved back there, and my sister

Noel and her family lived there too, along with most of the relatives I grew up with.

He said we could make a wonderful cross-country trip out of it, which we did. Once in Michigan, we lived with Noel until our newly built house was ready. I am so grateful to my sister and brother-in-law, David, for the kindness and support they showed me and the kids. I am fairly sure they, along with everyone else, thought Paul was a bit crazy. They never said much about it.

Soon after our arrival in Livonia, we moved into our new house and started to get settled.

Paul had talked a relative into letting us help them open a deli where my Aunt Suad would work as a cook. After we opened it and it was doing well, I got a high-paying executive job at Hudson's with benefits, and soon I was working long days. A few months later, Paul somehow managed to open a pizzeria in Whitmore Lake. I clearly wasn't paying close attention, and I have long ago taken responsibility for my part in that mess.

Paul was using credit cards that he had opened, forging my name, and he kept them hidden from me until the bitter end. That is when the sky started falling, bit by bit, damaging everything and everyone along the way.

We were about to lose everything and had to sell our house. Like all the other crazy things that were happening at that time, as soon as we listed our house, at a time when homes were taking forever to sell, we got an offer that was well over asking price.

A young man who had just won the Michigan lottery made that offer so his sister could go to Lady Madonna school right around the corner. It had been his mother's dream to send her daughter to Lady Madonna High School.

They bought the house with a cash offer, and we were able to move quickly. We headed back west to California and moved into Paul's family's house until we could get our bearings. Soon after we got back to Marin County, Paul had to file for bankruptcy. I was not on the bankruptcy filing with him, as advised by our attorney, due to other new developments. Ultimately, though, I was the one who paid all outstanding taxes and other expenses that were not part of the bankruptcy. It took me over eight years to pay everything off. Day by day, week by week, year by year, with my spreadsheet in hand; working as much as I could and obsessing over that next IRS payment.

The other shock to the system took place soon after we arrived back in Marin. I learned (rather my suspicions were confirmed) that Paul was bisexual. He was forced to tell me because he wasn't feeling well and had just tested positive for HIV. He had heard about a friend that was dying from Aids, and it turns out that Paul was intimate with him in the weeks before we moved to Michigan.

In those days, an HIV+ diagnosis was a death sentence, and for three years, I had to be tested every three months. The result was always negative, and I always thought of those results as my own personal lottery win.

Those were the toughest days of my life. Paul convinced me to tell no one because it would have a "negative impact on the kids," and I went along. It was so hard to carry that on my own and make excuses for Paul's illness and his inability to eat with us because the new medications made him so nauseous all the time. Even harder was the waiting for each test result, and I still get a pit in my belly when I think of the phone call from the doctor to tell me the result.

When I look back at that time, I believe that I survived having intense faith in the following: that I would never test positive, that I would leave Paul for the betrayals and the damage he had done in our lives, and I would find a new path forward. But that period of my life was so intensely painful for so many reasons, some of which are unbearable and still make me sad when I think about them.

At first, we separated. We did not get divorced so that Paul could keep his medical benefits that my work offered.

After the most difficult years of my life, I finally moved out. For several years, we lived as roommates before I finally left in 1996.

I never tested positive, and my name had not been on the bankruptcy because that attorney worried at that time that if I were to ever test positive, I might need to file on my own. Thank God that never happened.

So, in 1996. After much turbulence in my life and in my children's lives, which was the hardest part for me (It still makes me cry), I finally found my path forward to independence and calm.

When I was on my own, I was able to create a foundation on which to build a new way of life for me and my family. When I look back at this time, it seems to me that I took the best of my past with me and left the worst behind. I had matured with a deeper understanding of my role in my own life, which allowed me to put my best self forward as I stepped forward into new beginnings.

As I became more secure in my abilities and in my self-awareness, I started to see change as a powerful process in my journey. I recognized that I could be more of what I saw around me that I liked and respected. I met John that Autumn and he became my main focus and target in this regard. Just by being himself, he set the bar so much higher for me, and I am profoundly grateful for the friendship we developed.

For me, a balance and safe haven started to come into focus when he came into my life, first as a colleague, then a friend and business partner, and then a life partner. This beautiful period in my life felt almost miraculous as it slowly unfolded. With it came trust, respect, unconditional love, friendship, and safety. Something I wish for everyone. Something that I never understood, just how much I needed and yearned for. These basic rights of life, trust, respect, and safety have made me whole, and the abundance of it all has changed my perspective on many things. It was a conscious decision to accept the past for what it is and to embrace the future for what I wanted it to be. I was not regretful for my past and understood that it was all part of my journey and therefore part of me too.

As time marched on and in my newly found independence and self-confidence, I felt some change taking place in the workplace, too, or was it just in me?

Even though my confidence was boosted, so was my awareness. I am specifically talking about gender equality at work.

In this, there is much work left to do. I am still appalled at how many men in the workplace still don't see or hear women in the same way they see or respond to male colleagues. I've had to figuratively wear a hat every time I walk into a room with male colleagues. This hat protects me; it is my 'Hat of Assertion.' I've had to be extremely steadfast and assertive to hold my ground.

The grocery industry is where I built my career, and by sheer determination, I have gained much respect for my expertise and knowledge. I have learned to mitigate the discrimination and keep it at bay for the most part. I had to speak louder, more often, and accomplish more than every male colleague. I had to sit through hundreds of meetings where one of the men would put forth an idea that I had suggested weeks or months before and take credit for it. A woman can only protest so much before being looked at as caddy or credit seeking. I did my fair share, though, as this was insanely frustrating. Standing my ground was a lot of work all of the time, and in the end, the people that reported to me were my focus because they were where I was making the most difference.

That saying, "it's not easy being green" ... I remember hearing Kermit the Frog from the Muppets sing this for the first time and vividly thinking that I could relate because it's not easy being a girl. It became my swan (frog) song...

This has been a central theme in my entire life. I absolutely love being female (and the color green), and even though I have endured challenges, I am so grateful to know that things are better for my daughters, Elise and Sonia, and my granddaughters, Audriana, Amina, and Alma. They are fierce, and that is mostly a tribute to their mothers and fathers. Bit by bit, generation by generation, I have seen improvements in my lifetime, but I wonder if we can fully change the balance of what seems like a biological dominance that *some* men feel over women. Is it something that will always exist? Intellectually, men can aspire to elevated and equal relationships with women; I know many extraordinary men who are proof of this.

In the end, though, it seems to me that it is still a man's world. I aspire to a world where a woman experiences a workplace and a home where she is safe and is treated as an equal. I pray for a change for good, when equality for all women and girls becomes not just an ideal, but a reality.

PARENTS

Parents

Growing up, I was closer to my father than my mother. I loved hanging around with dad, following him around, and being his right-hand gal. As much as I love the kitchen and cooking as an adult, from my earliest age, I enjoyed my dad's world more than anything. The simple fact is that when I was young, I enjoyed the outdoors more than cooking and more than what was happening in the house and my dad spent most of his time outdoors when he was not working.

When he was home, he would always be working on a project, most of them outdoors. The fact that he was the one who took us to the park most of the time was also motivation to be around him. Being with him and my sisters in the park was the most wonderful part of the day.

I was eager to help him with all of his projects. Dad had no sons, and I used to wonder if he thought having a son would have given him a more traditional helper with projects, but I was happy to fill that role in my own girly way.

As far back as I recall, it was clear to me that the girls in our culture were intended to be domestic, to make sure the menfolk were taken care of, and to know how to cook and clean. It's funny to say that now, as it seems so outdated. These customs changed quickly within my own lifetime. I can look back and easily see how the old ways from the country they left behind started mingling with the American norms. Life was just changing in general, and women's roles were evolving.

I imparted the values and sensibilities that I grew up with to my children, and it was always my hope that they would maintain the core traditions and best of the Palestinian culture while cultivating new possibilities. That is exactly what happened. I couldn't be prouder of their love of family, kindness, and of their education and accomplishments.

We all grow up learning from our parents the way around life within our family dynamic, and from there, and from generation to generation, the path continues.

I was around eight when I started paying more attention to my mom and the kitchen. When I was old enough to understand the competition between my mother and my aunts about who could make the best Palestinian dishes, I became extremely interested, as I too have a competitive streak. It seemed to me much like a game. I enjoyed listening to them bicker about this ingredient and that ingredient and how long to cook a dish. There were endless nuances to each dish, and endless conversations ensued.

I found this fascinating, and at around 10 years old, I began to figure out a way to impress everyone with my own food skills. This involved the styling of our Palestinian dishes.

Looking back, I don't think making an impression was truly my objective, but rather a desire to be seen by my parents and also to make our beautiful foods shine even more brightly.

I became quite enamored with the idea of dressing up the dish of rice or the dish of lamb. I thought that many of our dishes were brown in color and lacked vibrancy. I started thinking of ways to bring color to the plate and of the appropriate and complementary vegetables and garnishes that would make the dish look more beautiful. Since we all loved crisp and fresh green onions to munch on with our meal, I would lay two or three long and perfect green onions alongside the *hashwa* on the platter and add a couple of wedges of tomato or a radish. I would rim the platter of lamb with roasted garlic bulbs, sprigs of fresh thyme, and lemon wedges. Nothing earth-shattering, but my parents and relatives noticed, and it became a topic of conversation. At first, they laughed and joked about how adorable my new talent was, and later, they came to truly embrace it.

Our meals usually boast a number of varied dishes and when I garnished them it was important to me to consider the collective visual of all the dishes together as they were lovingly laid out. The garnish had to make sense with the entire banquet and not take away from the customs but rather elevate the sensory experience.

I believe the family's acknowledgment for my compulsion to garnish fueled my desire to cook and to present the food for my family and later for friends and for customers by way of my future catering business.

It was of the utmost importance that I didn't simply adorn one of our cherished dishes; it was imperative that I learned how to make them as well. My mother was the best Palestinian cook I have ever known, and I am quite certain that she became this way out of love for her family and also because she wanted to be the best amongst her cousins, sisters, sisters-in-law, and some of the aunts that she looked up to.

I think my mom and I have this in common, but for as long as she cooked, my mom always maintained her 1st place in the cooking of our Palestinian dishes. She was always better than I and all my sisters, as I am sure they would agree.

Her cooking was one of her greatest sources of pride, only second to the pride she exuded for her beautiful girls and all of her grandchildren.

When it comes to cooking our food, my daughter might

say the same of me. When it comes to cooking any other dishes, I don't think that would be the case, as she seems to rise above my skill set with other dishes.

My son Jameel's food magic lies within his exquisite palate for all food. He can spot a substituted ingredient with one bite! And he is sure to tell me about it too. He understands the nuance of seasoning like no other. I have a profound respect for his palate and love to cook for him. I know most parents love to cook for their children, and for me, it's the greatest joy to take food to the table for the ones you love, and when they appreciate it to the point of giving feedback, even a critique, it's even more rewarding. The fact that they pay attention to the art of food and the treasures that come with eating together means everything to me. As parents themselves, they are now carrying this forward, and mealtime is important in their homes.

As much as I grew to love being in the kitchen, on any day of the week when my dad wanted to be outside or working on a project, I would be there.

I miss him still and all of his quirky ways and quirky fixes. I love to tell the story about how I found him in the garage one day, pounding screwdrivers into the wall. I asked him why he was doing that, and he said he needed some really big nails to hold heavy things and that he had lots of screwdrivers but no big nails! After that day, you would see the row of screwdrivers pounded into the wall with any random number of garage things hanging from them. He was magical in this way, and I am so grateful that I have that uncanny ability to make do with what's on hand just like he did. It's not always perfect, but this mindset creates a canvas for creativity and thinking outside the box.

Over time, it has become apparent to me that the end

result of my particular blend of mother and father has had a very particular influence on my life.

An example of the blend: while I love to cook all foods; only when preparing the Palestinian dishes, I do not deviate from the recipes, nor the traditions associated with them, just like my mom did. Most everything else I cook is approached with freestyle and at times a wildly quirky plan, just like my father.

As life marched on and the years passed, I remained closest to my father. For me, he was the one with whom I easily and naturally enjoyed interacting with. I could talk about the grocery business, which became the industry I worked in, too, and he knew and understood what I was talking about. He was delighted in and fully contributed to these conversations. My father's temperament was much more like mine, and he never gave a lick of care about what anyone thought. My mom, on the other hand, was not like that, and so we didn't always see eye to eye about things when she was motivated by what others thought.

Since my father passed away, I have gotten closer to my mother. With my father gone, I still called most days and spoke with mom but mostly small talk about what the kids were doing. That being said, I still visit with my dad in my daily thoughts and dreams, and he will forever remain my number one. Dad's kindness, constant thirst and wonder spoke to my heart in ways that heal and inspire at the same time.

But life is funny, and now, my mom and I have the sweetest and most affectionate moments filled with an unconditional love that is so comforting. This late-blooming relationship of love and respect fills my heart because she has shown me more affection in the last few years than in the 65 years that came before. Somehow the years with dementia changed her in profound ways; slowly over time she let go of the need to be right about everything and have the last word. She cares much more about what is right in front of her than what she was missing somehow. I love this reprieve for her, this transcendence into the here and now and to her looking into my eyes and seeing me, and me her.

Her one purpose in life these days is to hear about her children and grandchildren, and love seems to be her singular focus, with no cooking, cleaning, or other distractions to get in the way. Throughout life when we see photos of mom, she often looked serious, and she says that she has a terrible smile which is not true. Her smiles don't come that often but when they do they are priceless.

At Jameel's Berkeley Law School Graduation

MARRIAGE

Marriage

I married Jerry Harb in April of 1974, in San Francisco, California and here is how that came to pass. In 1972, just after my graduation from Bentley High, our family moved from Livonia, Michigan, to Millbrae, California. This is where I met Father Gregory. He was the priest at St. Nicholas Orthodox church in Diamond Heights, San Francisco. It was a beautiful church on a hill with a beautiful view. Majestic Orthodox icons adorned the inside, and a golden dome adorned the outside.

We lived close to Fr. Gregory and his family. I don't recall how, but somehow he learned that I love to sing. It didn't take long for him to invite me to join his church choir. I remember very clearly the day he took me to choir practice, and we drove into the city to St. Nicholas together. He never stopped talking the entire way; he was a giant personality… but that's a whole other story.

Choir practice was every Thursday evening, and that's where I met Jerry Harb and his mother, Jean Harb. They were both in the choir, she an alto like me, and Jerry a tenor with the most beautiful voice. The choir director was a kind but nervous man who was quite passionate about Byzantine music. He loved Jerry's voice so much that he always awarded him the solos.

This sets the stage for my eventual marriage to Jerry. He and I would see each other every Thursday evening at choir practice and then again every Sunday morning in the loft where we sang in the choir.

Like most churches, our church had a social hour after the service where everyone would visit. Jerry and I hit it off right away and became fast friends. He was super cute, super sweet, and sang like an angel. His voice was amazing, especially when he would sing the Byzantine hymns. He had the most supreme tenor falsetto that would give me goosebumps. When he was singing those ethereal songs everyone would stop and listen. He had a gift, and he played the piano beautifully as well. I loved to listen to him sing, enjoyed choir practice and especially learning all the beautiful Byzantine pieces of music.

Music had always been a huge part of my life, and I would lose myself in all manner of albums, playing them over and over again. My dad was always asking me to sing for him, not that I needed anyone to ask because I would just walk around singing. To this day, I remember the lyrics for every song that I ever loved. I'm always fascinated by that because I don't have such stellar recall for some other things.

Because of this love of music and the comfort I took from it, meeting Jerry was like finding a perfect new friend in a new place, and the shared love of music was familiar and welcomed. We hit it off immediately, and I knew he was happy to meet me, too. He was so sweet and kind, and we would talk about music and all of the musicians of the day. We loved to sing together, and soon I found myself looking forward to Thursdays and Sundays.

Several months later after Thursday choir practice, Jerry drove me up to the top of Twin Peaks, one of the tallest peaks in the city, offering incredible panoramic views of San Francisco and the bay when it was not covered in fog. This was a super clear night, and I had never seen the view from up there, and Jerry was excited to share it. We listened to Elton John on the way, and I learned about his great love for this artist. When we got to the top, we both got out of his Fiat and just stared at the amazing sights. There wasn't any romance in this little ride to the top of Twin Peaks, but it was romantic in its own way as it was filled with young ideas and brimming with excitement. I can still remember the heady feeling of having this new friend. It was a welcome balm after leaving my best friend Karen behind in Michigan and thinking that I would never find such a friend again.

Jerry and I talked and talked and played different songs and looked at the city below, trying to figure out which streets were which, and needless to say, I got home an hour and a half late that night, and our budding friendship got our fathers' attention, Shawky Mousa and Rizik Harb. These were two proud Palestinian men living large in San Francisco, and they were ready to take a stand on this relationship as it was unfolding.

Now, mind you, we lived in a culture where people loved to talk and gossip, and the young girl and the young boy spending time together was juicy gossip material indeed.

We would hang out at choir practice, and then we would spend time together on Sundays. My parents, especially my mom, did not like it because they were very worried about what people would say.

This was even more true as we were new to the San Francisco Bay Area Ramallah community, which included my future husband's family and so many new aunts, uncles, and cousins. My parents wanted to make a good impression with five daughters approaching marrying age in this new town. At that time, our ages ranged from 10 to 20 or thereabouts, and I think my mom imagined that all eyes were on us older daughters. The topic of marriage started in a girls late teens in those days, and sometimes even in the mid-teens.

With my family being so very new to the Bay Area, they wanted to get off to a great start without any gossip-related marks on our new reputation there. I can imagine with five daughters that there's a lot to protect. Within a few months of when Jerry and I met, the fathers got together and decided that if we were going to spend that much time together, we must get engaged. I remember my father talking to me about this in the family room on Madera Way. I remember looking outside while he was talking, and I was not really sure what to say or how to feel. In that moment, I remembered mom yelling at me the past Sunday for hanging out with Jerry after church, and that everyone was noticing. I was sure that prompted the talk dad was having with me at that moment.

Unbeknownst to me or Jerry, our fathers had gotten together and decided our future.

We had been in California less than a year, but by the time I left Michigan, my father had been asked at least twice that I know of for my hand in marriage. This started at the age of 15. I know that both of the boys were new to America and barely spoke English.

I was petrified in those days of what might come in the way of a husband.

To this day, I'm not sure why I thought I would just have to do whatever my parents said. I have heard it said that if you don't think you have a choice, it's just like not having a choice. Understanding you are free to make your own choices requires a level of maturity that I do not believe I possessed at that time.

There were other things happening at that same time,

too. In our new California Ramallah community, my eldest sister, Noel, was being pursued by an "American" boy, David, her high school sweetheart from Michigan. My parents were not happy with the prospect of their eldest child not marrying a "good boy from a Ramallah family." The arguments were endless, but in the end, they agreed because David came from a well-to-do, respected family, and because David was persistent and sincere in his love for my sister.

One time, when I was walking in the courtyard of Bentley High during a recess, I heard my sister's laughter, and when I looked to see where it was coming from, I could see Noel and David sitting close to each other by the open window in a classroom. They were completely engaged with each other, and I could see that look of love in their eyes. I remember feeling a little uneasy, too, like I was peeking into something private, but now I am grateful for that moment and that memory I have of their young love.

In the end, the "true love" marriage prevailed, not the semi-arranged marriage. Noel and David have celebrated 50 years together! Jerry and I made it to 11.

So, when my dad told me that he wanted me to marry Jerry, I agreed. What I specifically remember feeling was that if I were going to have to marry a Ramallah boy, Jerry was certainly going to be the best that would come my way. I already liked him, thought he was so cute and kind, and his musical talents were an incredible bonus that would surely make me happy. Thoughts of marriage and such things were confusing at best, and my naivety didn't offer any clarity. Everything seemed like it would be ok; after all, my parents wouldn't steer me wrong, and I even loved his adorable Fiat! I knew this marriage would make my parents happy, and that in a strange way it would help to ease their pain or discomfort of their eldest not marrying within the community. Also, I felt that I would at least be married to someone to whom I could relate. At that time, I told myself that my parents were not going to let their second daughter also marry an "American," so I went for it.

Jerry grew up in Torrance, CA., and was super modern. He was first generation like me, and our parents all grew up together in Ramallah. Things felt as they should, and I started to get excited. I remember standing alone in the backyard and singing love songs aloud and wondering what it would be like to be a bride. One time, when Jerry and I attended a church camp, we performed together at a talent show. Together we sang *Your Song* by Elton John, and this singular moment remains one of my favorite memories of our lives together.

There were lots of wedding plans in those days, one daughter getting married after the next. I was 19 when I got married and quite immature in so many ways. I remember standing in the nave of that church on the hill where I first met Jerry. I was in my beautiful white wedding gown and veil with my dad on my right arm. I don't recall one reflection on the magnitude of that moment, or for any of the moments that came before leading up to the day of marriage. I remember all the planning that was done by everyone else, and that the only thing that I needed to do was to look beautiful and be polite. And that I did. Standing in that nave with my dad. I remember thinking in such a childlike way that all of these people were here to see me, so pretty in my dress. Indeed, this is what I was feeling, and in such a disconnected way from what was truly taking place. I look back and attribute it to a lack of maturity, especially as it relates to understanding the profound meaning of marriage. I don't ever remember thinking about what I was actually about to experience in terms of a lifelong commitment to this person and what any of it really meant.

Since then, I have wondered if other young women with a similar betrothal experience as well as an insulated childhood must have felt disconnected too. I wonder if what felt to me like a stunted maturity was due to my parents' extreme strictness and my minimal experience and social interactions outside of my cousins. The first person I really dated was Jerry. I had a couple of crushes, but nothing ever truly materialized. I had no idea how to pursue a boy and was sure they wouldn't pick me. I saw the way they went after the blonde and red-haired girls and felt so outside of the inner circles of high school crushes.

I remember turning 16 and feeling bad that I had not had a first kiss. For some reason, I was so focused on this. I felt something surely must be wrong with me that I had not yet been kissed. Soon after that, I was allowed to go to a football game with Karen. I remember thinking it would be fun, but at that game, I found it boring and unfamiliar.

Karen drove, and we were supposed to drive home together, but she had been after the quarterback, Tom, for months, and the plans changed quickly.

After the game, Tom asked us if we wanted to go get some food. She got in the front seat with Tom while his best friend, Ron, got in the back with me. I didn't know much about Ron except that he seemed to have lots of girlfriends. Soon after we drove away, Tom pulled into a neighborhood, and I asked Karen where we were going. She turned and looked at me with a look that I took to mean, "It's ok, just go with it."

I knew she really liked Tom, and within moments, we were parked, and they were kissing. I felt panic and turned to look out the window when Ron reached over suddenly, grabbed me, and tried to kiss me. I was horrified by the assault; he smelled of beer, and his hands were grabbing my breasts. Within seconds, I got out of the car and ran most of the way home. The entire way home and for weeks afterwards, I thought how terrible it was for that to be my first kiss experience.

Later that year, I kissed a young Palestinian man. I liked him and the kiss, but his home was in Ramallah, and he wasn't moving to America anytime soon. He had been in Michigan at Wayne State University and was a friend of my uncle Basem's.

Time moved forward, and I do remember that kissing Jerry seemed natural, as if we were to be married. Together, we had two beautiful children, and Jerry and I still have a sweet friendship. Life is full of twists and turns, and that's what makes the journey an adventure... or visa versa.

Elise and Jameel with their dad in Oakland, CA, at Jameel and Sonia's Home. 2012

St. Nicholas Orthodox Church -Diamond Heights,
San Francisco, California. My view from the choir loft.
I was married here, and my children were baptized here.
So much of my family's new life in California
was centered on this church on top of the hill.

LOVED

Loved

I believe in a higher power, and I believe that this higher power is Love.

This love to me is at the center of the universe and is the most profound energy that has the ability to bring light to all things.

This is not to say that I do not believe in God; it is more to say that I believe God is love.

When love is the force behind actions, beautiful things happen. Love empowers and is the conduit for goodness in the world as we know it.

But what then of fear? I came to believe that fear is the opposite of love. I heard this many years ago, spoken by the great Joseph Campbell. I remember how intensely it resonated with me. It makes perfect sense to me that the opposite of love is fear because fear drives hatred and bias, and thus many undesirable actions that lack empathy. I think that a lack of empathy occurs when fear trumps love.

My belief in this concept has brought great humility to my life and also a deeper understanding and insight into the darkness where some people live.

Love brings joy and nurturing. When it is shared and experienced, it can foster growth. Fear and hatred bring fear and hatred right back to the hater, and it seems impossible to break this destructive cycle and the pain that it creates. To take this a step further, I believe this highest power of love, when embraced, becomes part of our very being, contributing to a kindness engine of sorts that propels a joyous and compassionate human experience. I have lived my life in this place as often as possible, and an inner peace and light rest in my soul. When I have felt anger and even hate, I have recognized the tumult and disgust I feel inside and do everything I can to let go of the darkness that creates those feelings.

The challenge, then, is to embrace ourselves and our fellow humans; every single one that we share an experience with. To embrace them even when they are burdened with fear and hatred. In doing so, we do our part to share the path of kindness and love, because I believe with my whole heart that love is the elixir that heals all wounds.

Jimmy Carter once said that a preacher told him that in their day-to-day interactions, that he loves God first, and after that he loves the person standing right in front of him.

Imagining this, one can quickly see how our thoughts and actions can change the outcomes of each human exchange.

The human journey is a culmination of experiences that cause us to have different perspectives on life as we move forward. For me, each experience is an opportunity to grow and to learn and to love ourselves and others more deeply.

When I think back on all the things I thought were so important when I was young, I have come to realize that my core values and beliefs haven't changed much at all. As a child, love and nurturing were all around me. Being part of a big family filled my world with many moments that taught me how to share kindness and love. Fear got in the way at times, but it never prevailed.

In the early years, for my dad and especially my mom, it seemed that the fear of all that was unknown in their new America was at times a barrier. It must have felt impossible to protect their children from that authentic fear and need for caution that I know they must have experienced.

With faith in family and with intention we found our way through all of that.

I have grown as a person and worked hard to bolster my best self and even harder to shed certain behaviors and attitudes that I found less desirable.

In the end, the biggest change for me has to do with true love. Being with a partner who loves, respects, and creates an environment of trust has allowed for the most meaningful change in my life.

In 1996, when I was 42 years old, I met John Honeycutt. We worked together, and when I first met him, he was my boss. I was immediately struck by his intentional and impeccable style of communication. Communication had always been a struggle for me. I don't really know why, but I always felt as though I wasn't explaining myself as well as I could, which caused anxiety and often led me to over-explain.

Growing up, I struggled to express myself and ended up pouring my feelings into my activities. I learned to excel at projects with my dad, to work and help in the store, and within the home, to cook and be really good at it. These things came easily to me. I always felt that my brain was thinking one thing, but my words weren't conveying the feelings or thoughts I had. I still struggle with this.

My mom had a passive aggressive way of speaking, and my dad kept to himself much of the time, so with this backdrop, one might imagine what a joy it was to meet someone who spoke quietly, plainly, and always with deep integrity. I grew up in a household with a lot of gossip, and some untruths in the vein of chatter were told. I have come to realize that many of these untruths were not malicious but rather told for entertainment.

My mother especially had a knack for telling people what they wanted to hear, whether it was the truth or not. One might think that a child wouldn't necessarily fall into the same patterns, but usually, children learn everything from their parents—the good, the bad, and the indifferent.

Learning for me was about seeing a different way. When I met John, I started to recognize that saying less is often a better choice. It has taken me many years to learn this, and I still work at it, but I have been able to watch, listen, and learn. Over time, I have felt the calm that a thoughtful conversation brings.

When John and I became romantically involved, I was struck by the devotion and respect he had for me as an equal. I had never felt such profound respect in my life. I can say unequivocally that it is the greatest joy to be loved unconditionally and to be respected for all that you are. You don't understand the deep value and healing that respect and truth brings until you experience it yourself. It really does set you free.

There are so many things about John that I love. He is kind, honest, and always says what he means and means what he says. He always does what he says he will do. If the landscape or circumstances change and he can't, he lets you know in advance and explains why.

John is fun-loving, loves to dance, play, and seek adventure. He loves the outdoors and is bound to nature, just like me. He is devoted to me and at times it makes me feel like the most important person in his world.

He's brilliant, an amazing partner, and can do pretty much anything he puts his mind to. I have felt a change in myself occurring slowly over time as the beauty of his spirit has intertwined with mine. It is a blessing, and I hope that I bring him as much joy as he brings me. I am forever grateful to have found such a human being. I hope every day that everyone finds that special person in their lives.

Indeed, John has a beautiful way about him, he is impeccable with his word, and that means so much to me. This is something I have always strived for, growing up in a family where words were like leaves flying in the wind—this way and that way. Sometimes the words were just words, without much substance. My dad used to tell my mom to 'stop with the empty talk.' He had a saying, and he would use it often, and of course, he would say it in Arabic, something like *hachee fathee…*

He didn't like gossip at all.

I believe in the old adage that you are who you hang out with. I like to be aware of my interactions and do my best to take the high road. It's important. This may seem like a small thing, but communication is fundamental to life and is ultimately related to the quality of one's life. I have learned so much about love, trust and communication from John and look forward to each day ahead as we journey on together.

Life is short and fleeting, and we leave behind a reputation and a legacy. I hope the memory of me is one of kindness and joy. Over time, and over generations, long after we are all gone, the stories will change, but the essence of a life is forever held in the universe.

John and Me

On the roof in Marin, 2016

CHILDREN

Children

I have two beautiful children, and I don't know how the time has passed so quickly. Precious magnificent moments passed and they went from babies to adults.

People always tell you this will happen when you're a new mother. "Gosh, enjoy every moment, the time flies by!" You can hear it a thousand times, but it doesn't ring true until it actually happens to you. It is a constant refrain even as time marches on and they are older. It's the elusive, the preciousness of life that slips away minute by minute, day by day.

My own life too, I feel it; the quickness of the passage of time, and yet with all of it's fleeting, I live with a full heart and a profoundly deep awareness and appreciation for what is here now.

My children; my babies were so tiny and cradled so close, and now they are parents who cradle their own children. I'm certain that they experience this fragility too. The unbridled joy of the new heartbeat that is yours and the fullness of each moment that is always on wing, and then each and every particular sweetest of moments is gone forever, never to be repeated. That one sweet moment where the heavens open up and grab hold of your heart and then that moment is gone forever.

The love, the joy, and yes, the ache in my heart when I think about my children and now my grandchildren is unlike any other feeling. It resides there in my heart like a bookmark for all the pages of this beautiful road I walk with them. One day, our days together on earth will end, and yet we will never part ways.

My children have given me a love and a light that is eternal.

Both of my children are my finest works of art. It sounds crazy to say it that way, but that's how I feel. As we age, we think of what we will leave behind, what we contributed while we were here; our legacy. I am so blessed to have been given the gift of Elise and Jameel, and all that followed them into my universe.

Each of my children is extraordinary in every way to me. I know most parents will say this.

I do say it and I think it, every day. I believe wholeheartedly that they are genuinely kind, brilliant, and fully engaged in their precious lives. They have abundant lives with beautiful families of their own, and they are happy, and they love each other and would protect each other fiercely. I don't think a mother can ask for anything more.

From the early days of my parenting, other mothers would ask me for advice. When my children were little, other mothers would ask me things like, "They eat so well; how do you do it?" "They're so well-behaved; how do you do it?" "They're so sweet to their grandparents and other children; how do you do it?" "They're so neat and tidy; how do you do it?" Of course, I would share my day-to-day strategies, but I honestly didn't think much of it at the time. I started to recognize that the way I parented my children was not so similar to what I saw with other mothers my age. Let us remember that I was a young mother indeed for at 22, I already had sweet Elise.

I think the biggest difference was that I did not scold my children in front of each other or anyone else. I showered them with pure and unconditional love. Beyond these two pillars of my motherly knowledge, I also praised them for every positive trait that I witnessed.

Regarding children's schedules that mothers talk so much about, I did have specific timelines that I adhered to throughout their days. I also wanted them to eat all-natural, home-cooked foods, and was very strategic in how I introduced them to different foods.

Another particularly important influence that I was mindful of had to do with elders. In our culture, being kind and respectful, especially to elders, was an absolute requirement. My children learned this at an early age, as we spent a lot of time with grandparents and family.

Regarding the neat and orderly traits they developed, let's just say that I am unabashedly neat. When it comes to my environment, I am an asthete who loves a pleasing and serene home. I like the calm that comes from tidiness, as opposed to the chaos I sometimes felt and still feel when disarray floods a room. I can take it in small doses, but it's just not for me.

I am a little obsessive to be sure, but that's fine by me, as I think overall it has served me well. Both of my children must have learned quickly that this is the way things need to be. It's interesting to see the habits your children learn from you. I certainly learned about neatness from my mom. Keeping things so tidy might make some wince a little, but if they get the same pleasure I do from the neat and tidy gene, then it's all good!

As my children grew and thrived in their lessons and experiences, I was always asked for advice, but the questions were changing. "Why are your kids so good at school?" "Why are your kids so thoughtful?" "How did you do it?"

The advice I always gave was the same: When they're doing something wonderful, get out of their way and praise them. When they're acting in a way that causes concern or that you simply don't like, take them aside and speak to them in private about what they're doing and why they're doing it. Ask questions, listen, and help them see a better way. Honestly, the latter rarely happened.

I also have another golden rule that I believe to be missing in much of the parenting I have witnessed over the years. This is the rule of self-guided responsibility and intent. It is so important to let a child find their own way and be responsible for their own stuff.

A few examples: I rarely helped them with their homework, I didn't set curfews, and I didn't lecture.

I came from a place of expectation. I expected them to do their absolute best at all times. Simple but powerful.

This expectation I had for myself as well. This was how I lived my life, and it was woven into the fabric of their world every day. Not to say that I did not make mistakes, and I certainly did, but I always tried to do better. As children, they watched me and saw that my day was full of work and everything else that came after work. Day after day, I just did my absolute best—at least 110%, I would say. That is what I expected from them. I did not instruct them on how to reach that 110%; I just set the example and let them know when they were doing a great job.

When they exhibited enthusiasm or positive emotions about their accomplishments, I paid attention and praised them. If I thought something could have been improved in some way, I would say something like, "How do you like it?" or "Did it turn out the way you wanted?"

But let us not forget good fortune. I think luck is definitely at play here as well, but every time I say that to my mom or my sisters, they respond with something like, "I don't think so, you're an awesome mother." I certainly like to think that I am, and when I look back, I do see wonderful moments of motherhood, but I also believe there was plenty of room for improvement.

In the end, I think most parents do with what they have and with what they know. Circumstances differ for us all. Parenting is ideally a two-person job, and not every child has two parents who are present or fully engaged. Not all parents have the amazing support group I had in my mother, my father, and my big Palestinian family. Not all parents have the means to raise healthy, educated children. Not all parents have the luxury to tell a happy story about their children's lives.

A life story has a beginning, a middle, and an end, and I have been blessed with my beautiful children for most of my story, and for this, I thank the Heavens.

Having my children so young has given me a lifetime of divine joy, and I know I will leave the world a better place because of them.

Elise and I at Limantour Beach, California, on my 6oth birthday

Jameel and I at Mom and Dad's on Thanksgiving 2011

MUSIC

Music

As long as I can remember, I have loved music, and it has been my memory-making machine. I cannot think of any song without it being attached to some moment in time.

My mom and dad both loved music too. Dad would always put the radio on when he was working in the house, in the store, or hanging out in the garage. We listened to a lot of Arabic music at home and at our family parties (*haflas).* Mom played her Arabic songs while she was cleaning the house or getting showered and ready for the day. I am quite sure that felt quite luxurious to her when we were all grown and out of the house, and she had this precious solo time. As an adult, when I visited her in Michigan I would see her prancing around, in her underwear dancing to Fairuz while she did her makeup.

My mental library of music is a lot like my pantry, filled with the basic and essential goods, and with some more exotics to spice things up. I grew up with the beautiful and transportive sounds of Fairuz and Abdel Halim Hafez. These two artists in particular were favorites of my parents, and when my parents played this music, I felt like they brought the songs of their beloved Ramallah into our home. Nothing makes me feel connected to the love they had for their homeland as much as when I listen to this music.

My earliest memory of falling in love with a different and new kind of music was surrounded by the film West Side Story. After I saw that movie, it was all I could think about, and I quickly memorized every song. The movie was something quite wonderful and it spoke to my first-generation experience and the fear and fire many immigrants must have felt as they made their way through roads less traveled. There was so much for me to love about the story, but at the top of it all was the amazing soundtrack by Leonard Bernstein and Stephen Sondheim.

From that pivotal point, and with every subsequent movie I experienced, the soundtrack was always the highlight. Of course, there were albums and 45s, and we had a Hi-Fi, so it was one musical session or season after another. For anyone that doesn't know what a Hi-Fi is… in the 60s, a home Hi-Fi stereo console was state-of-the-art audio. I felt so lucky that we had one and played all of our records as often as possible. I can't look back at my childhood and teens without being immersed in a musical period of whatever I was listening to at the time.

Watching my grandchildren, Audriana, Amina, Alma, and now Khalil brings maximum joy as I see how much pleasure they get from music. From their first moments and through their young years I sang to them as often as possible and especially at bedtime when I was lucky enough to be with them at bedtime. I love to sing, so they hear *Tayta's* songs even as they grow older. Their parents have music playing in their homes as it is an essential pastime, so music is a daily experience.

I can see how music brings freedom of expression and even a kind of rapture to people. Maybe I'm projecting, but that's how I feel when I am listening to music; sometimes it knocks me down. I must stop what I am doing and just be in the moment. The world stops except for me and the music.

Recently, I went to see Hamilton at the Rodgers Theatre in New York with Jameel, Sonia, Audriana, and Amina.

Sitting with them so close to the stage was exciting beyond measure. The performance was electrifying, the writing magnificent, and sitting there in the grace of the love I feel for my family made that day one I will cherish for the rest of my days. Magical and brilliant at the same time, it stirred that same intense joy I had as a teen watching and listening to West Side Story, where it all started for me. Turning to my left to see Amina rapping to every song and then turning to my right to see wide-eyed Audriana absorbing all the dance moves and the brilliance of the theatre, was dreamy. And just beyond Audriana, my beautiful Sonia and Jameel… all of us together in this exceptional experience.

In Hamilton, the telling of the story about a painful history through the lens of the beautiful movement, brilliant singing, and dialogue, reached the audience in profound ways.

A few months later, on another Brooklyn visit, we were driving in Manhattan, and Audriana and Amina were in the back seat. Their dad and mom always let them request songs they want to listen to. Each gets a turn picking, even mom and dad. The girls chose "Satisfied" from Hamilton, a boisterous rap at a thrilling pace. I turned on my video and captured them rapping and acting out the entire song, all while sitting in the back seat. My heart was so full.

Later, back in San Francisco, I let Alma watch the video of her talented cousins, and she was all smiles and did not blink the entire time. We had to watch it several times.

And every time I sing to my youngest grandchild Khalil, he kicks and wiggles his entire body, rubbing his chubby little feet together with so much happiness. These moments will be gone soon but with every gift of a new day, a new musical possibility and experience emerges.

Growing up near Motown and working in the back room of my father's store, we would listen to songs, and I would memorize them. I think Motown and soundtracks are the two genres that truly fueled my intense desire to sing. It was definitely an escape for me; I could drown out some of the sounds and feelings of growing up in a big Palestinian family. At times, the household was intense, and music was one of my escapes. I would turn up the volume, and suddenly everything was about Motown or soundtracks and the myriad of stories and lives being lived in those songs. This music was also one of the ways I connected with my American self.

Part of my childhood was elevated to new heights when my father enjoyed listening to me sing. So often he would ask me to sing him a song. He would announce the song like ordering something from a menu. What a thrill that was. I loved to sing, and when a parent asks you to sing them a song, it is pretty special indeed. In those days, I would walk over to our Hi-Fi and select the requested album and sing my heart out. He was sitting in his chair, smiling, and bopping his head or tapping his foot. These were some of my favorite singing moments. When I fell in love with Barbra Streisand, was when Dad was asking me to sing the most. He would call her "Boorbara," which, amusingly is an Arabic sweet pudding-like dessert. After seeing Funny Lady, I learned every word of that soundtrack and I still know the words by heart to this day. He and I shared a love for Boorbara and thought her voice to be heavenly. Her voice is the first time, I though of the human voice as an instrument. Dad and I would talk about how it was that she could sing so perfectly and hit all this notes and hold the notes for so long. We were star struck.

In my teenage years, I fell in love with so many of the

folk artists of the '60s. I listened to Joni Mitchell, Neil Young, The Band, Laura Nyro, and other poetic artists like Joe Cocker. Leon Russel, Joan Baez, Bob Dylan, Leonard Cohen and Emmylou Harris. Hundreds of artists found their way into my heart and into my way of thinking, as music can do. In some ways, the songs of my teenage years informed some of my beliefs. An example of this is the Circle Game by Joni Mitchell. From the moment I heard that song, I felt a deep understanding of the circle of life and the fragility of time, and that song became an emblem for life, like a tattoo on my heart. I sang that song to my children, and now I sing it to my grandchildren.

Music was playing in my room or in our home most of the time, and when music became available to listen to with earplugs and to take with you, everything changed. I have loved walking forever, and taking the songs with me on my walks gave me a certain serenity, and I felt renewed by the time I got back or wherever it was I was going. Taking a stroll around the block with my music made the walks lively and full of emotion.

During my twenties and onward I attended many concerts and have distinct memories of what my life was like when I would go to those concerts. There is just something about music that can make time stand still and allow us a window from which to take a personal inventory, and somehow that data gets saved, or it did for me anyway.

Seeing Elton John, for example, will always bring images of my early married life to Jerry and to our young children, and of Jerry playing the piano for them - Elton John, of course! I recall the smiles and the laughter as they tried to play along with him.

Concerts bring back eras, not moments. My first concert

was Joe Cocker at Cobo Hall in Detroit. I remember the great anticipation I felt while we were driving up the circular driveway into the garage of that arena. I remember thinking that I was going to learn all of his songs and add them to my repertoire, but once he was on stage and shook so fiercely while he sang, as was his style, I forgot about all of that because I was mesmerized by this strange performer. I never saw anyone like him since.

I have been to so many concerts and loved them all, but if I had to choose, I would say the U2 concerts were some of my favorites. I love U2 and I attended almost all of those concerts with my dearest friend Siobain. We had the best times at those concerts, and we would compare how close we were to Bono from one concert to the next. Siobain was always great at getting the best tickets.

One special concert that stands out was when I saw Cat Stevens in Oakland. His music was so poetic and peaceful, an experience that was quite different than most, much louder concerts of the day.

I also feel so lucky to have seen Leonard Cohen in concert. John and I attended one of his last concerts in San Jose and made the long trip because we both love him and knew it would most likely be one of his last performances, and in fact, it was.

Seeing the Rolling Stones at Candlestick Park, Stevie Ray Vaugh in a small venue in Palo Alto, and Van Morrison in San Mateo were heady for sure. It snowed the night Jerry, and I saw Stevie Ray Vaughn. Pablo Cruise opened for him, and I thought that to be such a strange match up. It snowed the entire ride home from Palo Alto to Millbrae, where our children were staying with my parents. Snow in California is not an everyday sight, and it was quite magical. So many concerts that it would be impossible for me to recount them all. The Boss, the Stones, Boorbara, and more recent loves like Billie Eilish and Coldplay.

When I lived in Marin County, California, I worked at a recording studio as a Chef. It was a dream come true because I was able to cook while listening to live music by some of the best performers of the day. Pearl Jam, Linda Ronstadt, Hootie & The Blowfish, to name a few. I also met Keith Richards and will never forget answering the front door and seeing him standing there. Linda Ronstadt liked my food so much that she had me come cook for her at her home in Pacific Heights in San Francisco. She even says a special thanks to me on her Winterlight album.

I could go on, but now I find myself reminiscing about the music and the magic with each memory of these amazing concerts and the things that were happening in my life at those times. I love looking back at my life through the songs and the artists that fed my soul daily.

Elise, Jameel, and I have shared many good times talking about, listening to, and sharing music. Their playlists have always been favorites of mine.

Music is a human magnet. It pulls you in and doesn't let go. When I hear a song I love, I can hardly think of anything else. One of my fondest memories of this magnetic and powerful force happened when I was in Eze, France, walking down a cobbled, narrow, winding alley. After walking to the top of Eze to take in the view of the French Riviera, with my friend Stephanie we made our way back down. Suddenly, the voice of Leonard Cohen wafted through the air, and I followed the music into a small open door where a jewelry maker lived and worked. I ended up buying some green earrings just to stay and listen to this new Cohen work, "10

New Songs" that was playing in his workshop. I purchased that CD at the airport on my way home.

I can't imagine a life without music. To me, music is poetry, harmony, and storytelling. I never cared much for loud rock or subsequent loud genres that followed. I craved being able to hear the words and understand the story. What is life if not a story? When you add melody and harmony to storytelling, it becomes magical, an intoxicating elixir that is transformative, even if just for a few moments.

When Siobain and I both sang in the Winifred Baker Chorale of Marin, we had so much fun doing that together. The hardest piece we had to learn was Balthazar's Feast by William Walton. Once I did some research, once I had a better understanding of the piece, the music became so much easier to master.

Listening is an obvious choice for enjoying music, but I also love music for dancing. Once the music starts, even if the song has words, a good rhythm will win me over, and the dancing begins.

Whether listening or dancing, whenever I think of music, memories come to life. As much as I miss my dad, I always hear him through my songs and will never forget singing for him while he sat in his chair and drank his coffee. And my beautiful mother pressing play on her little CD player to listen to Fairuz while she did her chores. I cherish the memory of her smile and her lightness on her feet while she was serenaded by her majestic Fairuz.

I hope that my children and grandchildren will all live a life in the divine appreciation of music and the joy it brings, and I think this is a perfect moment to send my gratitude out to the universe for all the musicians who have brought me so much joy and enrichment. Music, like all art, is healing, inspiring, and provocative all at the same time. When you find music you love and share it with people you love, humanity shines more brightly.

My beautiful Elise and best friend Siobain at Domaine Chandon, June 2015. Vivaldi's Spring from the Four Seasons was playing in the background.

QUESTIONS

Questions

My parents taught me many things. I do not know where to start. A child watches and learns, and some children ask lots of questions. That was me. My father was right when he would say that I "came out asking questions." I can remember being this way with my father, my mother, my aunts, my uncles and at times, some of my sisters. My small life was filled with family, and a vast and almost endless list of people and situations to learn from. Lucky and loved was I.

Growing up, I definitely had a strong inclination toward what I call "elderly worship." I believed that everyone older than me knew a lot more than I did and so the questions were a part of my everyday life. It makes sense, right?

I liked to sit and listen to what all the elders were talking about. So much good information came my way via this pastime. They spoke of things that I could use in my everyday life like the best way to carve a watermelon or why you could see the stars better in the suburbs than in the city.

But mostly I asked lots of questions. If I wanted to know something, I asked a question. My questions began with "Why?" I was interested in why things happened, why we wanted to do a thing a certain way, and why one thing worked differently from another. Why were we going a certain route or why we were going to a new store or why one of my cousins didn't come to a party? And for more conceptual or scientific information, I was only satisfied if I received a thorough explanation. I always wanted to understand the history of and the innovation behind things.

My father was similar in his curiosity and his unabashed eagerness to fix anything and take risks in life.

His immigration to America at a young age is an expression of his courage. He wanted to explore possibilities. He was driven by knowledge and had a constant thirst for it. I don't mean in the more traditional sense of college and degrees; this was not who he was. Maybe he was just too busy making a living for his quickly growing family in America, and pursuing a formal education was not his priority.

My father wasn't the most disciplined man, and impulsive at times but a constant was his acute desire to learn. A testament to this is when he bought that set of encyclopedias and read every volume from front to back. In our grocery stores, he was always reading magazines that were for sale, learning as much as he could before the vendor came in and switched them out. I always noticed how he didn't care which magazine it was; in fact, I think he gravitated to whatever looked like something he knew nothing about. This is where his thirst lived, learning something new.

He also asked lots of questions in his very personal and charming way. I always loved watching him chat with his customers and vendors alike, asking questions, and always taking away some nuggets of information.

I inherited his thirst for knowledge, and it has served as a driver for a lifetime of growth and experience. I learned a lot from my dad, and what I learned from both my mother and father was very practical and important for a good and productive life. That being said, I'm fairly sure all my questions have annoyed many along my journey.

My mother was always the smartest person in the room, and in part this is because she had a sharp memory and, as a young girl, she read every free minute she had. From what she tells me, growing up in Ramallah with so many brothers, she, and her younger sister Siham had lots of free time because all the brothers were expected to do most of the chores. She chose reading with any free time she had, she tells the story where she would find the quietest most hidden corner in which to read undisturbed for as long as she could get away with it.

Of course, I learned many things from each of my parents. Each parent offering up different segments of knowledge with quite different styles and sensibilities. I use the word segments intentionally because for example; if I wanted to learn about oranges, they would each tell me different things and share different memories or ideas about an orange and by the end of my quest of the orange I had enough "segments" to make whole the orange of information that I was after.

I felt lucky to have this unending flow of information all around me. All I had to do was start asking the questions. Of course, there were times when I was brushed off but that was okay because I just came back a little while later. In the early days especially, there was always so much content to draw from because my parents themselves were learning new things every day about this new land they had come to call home. It's hard to put into words what this means, but any first-generation person reading this may make the connection and know exactly what I mean. My mom and my older sister, Noel, had only been in America for about a year before I was born, so my early years were spent exposed to their emergence into their new America. My dad had been in America a little longer. As a child in Detroit and then when we moved out to the suburbs, everyday life was filled with the new found situations and the new ways to live life.

I believe they were keenly aware of the unique new experiences they found themselves in as they moved through their day-to-day activities in a brand-new world. If you think about it, learning through this duality of old world vs new world and at a necessary accelerated rate is the way of life for anyone who immigrates to a new country.

The person traveling the two roads; the old ways and the new ways creates a conduit for wonder and can establish an insatiable appetite for knowledge and security, not just for your new home but for precisely how one fits into this new home. There was the tension of the message, too, spoken and many times unspoken, to be "careful" around the "Americans." This unintentional passing on of fear and of the unknown can take a toll on a child. This sometimes left me with feelings of confusion and a deep need for a better understanding of what this all meant.

Fortunately for me, our day-to-day living and learning from aunts, uncles, and cousins were a constant, and what I learned from this amazing collection of people filled my spirit with immeasurable satisfaction, security and an understanding of how things worked. For this, I am grateful. My life was built around my amazing Palestinian American family that offered so much community, companionship, and learning every day. I had many loving people around to answer my unending questions.

The domestic and the practical; these are the things I learned early in life. They may not be heady or newsworthy, but they are great things that have brought me joy and harmony. Most of what I learned, if not all, by the age of five was learned from a Palestinian, and what an incredible gift to have been able to saturate my whole self in this beautiful culture and knowledge that was passed on.

This treasure trove of knowledge had much to do with how to create a good life filled with family, security, and warmth. Freedom, kindness toward others, and having enough to eat are the simple and poignant cornerstones of my life yet truly the finest diploma any human could receive.

My parents and the elders in our family also taught me to understand that this diploma for the human experience should be available to everyone who walks the earth. After all, we have nothing without freedom, kindness, and a warm meal at the table with our loved ones and a soft place to rest our bodies when the day is done.

Jannette Salwa Dirbas (on the right)
Ramallah, Palestine circa 1949

Shawky Jamil Mousa Ramallah, Palestine circa 1947

ADVENTURES

Adventures

When I was 62, John and I went to Kauai. While we were there, we decided to take the trek up to the Sacred Falls in Wailua River Park. We were warned that it was not an easy hike, but we decided to give it a try anyway. We were also told that not everyone makes it all the way to the falls, but we were determined. It was an adventure from the start, as we had to rent a kayak, load it onto our car, offload it at the river, and then kayak to the base of the ascent to the falls. So far, so good...

The kayak trip was peaceful and relaxing, as we meandered along the beautiful Wailua River. Little did we know what was ahead. Looking back now, I realize that although the kayaking seemed strenuous at the time, it was the easy part. Once we reached base camp, we had to pull our kayaks onto the shore, and that is when we encountered the mud… deep, thick, and relentless! It made sense given that we were on a riverbank, but in those first moments of my muddy experience, I didn't fully comprehend what this 'mud' would mean for our impending hike.

We were told to only take what we could carry, as we'd need our hands free. These words of advice were definitely a sign of what was to come. We made our way up to a gathering spot where about 40 people were waiting, all ready to start the hike to the Sacred Falls. Our guide led the way, explaining that he'd only accompany us part of the way and that he'd share what to expect as we continued on our own.

The area was heavily forested, with vines hanging from the trees that ended up being essential for our trek. It was dense, humid, and offered the narrowest of paths lined with vines, roots, rocks, and all kinds of organic materials. Our feet and hiking sandals were already weighed down with thick mud. We lost a couple of hikers during this leg of the journey, and the bugs were a bit of a bother. But soon, I stopped noticing them, as I had bigger things to worry about.

After about 45 minutes of hiking, we came to the point where we had to cross the river. We lost another dozen or so adventurers at this point. The river was wide, deep, fast, and filled with large mossy boulders. A rope stretched across the river, and that's how we were expected to cross. In hindsight, I'm not sure why I didn't turn back with so many others. Even though I was somewhat terrified, I was having fun. It was an adventure after all, and John was cheering me on. He convinced me that I could do it, so we pressed on.

Into the river I stepped and remember holding onto that rope midway across and feeling the rush of the current beneath my feet. The rope was sturdy, and the cool water felt wonderful as it washed away all the mud. This was just the incentive I needed to keep moving. I took it one step at a time, with John beside me, and we made it across. I felt elated, like I had already accomplished so much. But little did I know, the toughest part was still ahead. Now, we had no guide, and only six of us were left.

Once we crossed, the ascent became moderate to difficult, and the heat was intense. The biggest challenge was the mud—our feet sank six to eight inches with every step, making it exhausting to pull our feet out and move forward. If I didn't step in the middle of the muddy path, I had to navigate the slippery, tripping hazards on the sides. I kept repeating the guide's advice in my head: "Stay in the channel on the path where people have hiked before," and that's exactly what I did.

This part of the trek took about another hour, with constant obstacles and challenges. Occasionally, we found small clearings, which made it easier, but coming across the deep gouges in the earth created by foraging wild boars were a constant reminder of the potential danger lurking nearby. The fear of a wild boar attack lingered in my mind, but I just kept moving.

Finally, we heard the falls in the distance. The sound was magnificent music to our ears, and I remember John turning to me with a smile when he heard it too. As the booming sounds grew louder, we turned a final corner, and there they were—the majestic Sacred Falls. To our surprise, there were about twenty people there, including children, resting, and picnicking on massive boulders. Others were swimming and frolicking under the falls, clearly having made the same challenging journey because the path we took was the only way to get there.

We found our spot and sat happily and delighted in our much-anticipated picnic. We basked in the mutual satisfaction shared by the other travelers. After some rest, it was time to experience the falls up close. Crawling up over more slippery green rocks and jumping into the water was harder than expected, but it was an absolute thrill. I still remember the intense joy and excitement of being tossed around by the falls. Being there with John in that exquisite moment is an unforgettable experience, and one I'll always be grateful for.

The funny thing is, I barely remember the way back.

There were many other adventures, but this one was supreme as it pushed me into the unknown to face new challenges that I was so elated to meet. Overcoming the fear and the exhaustion was transformative and truly tested my resilience.

May 2017 - The Hike to Sacred Falls in Kauai, Hawaii

ART

Art

Artists and art help to make up the ethereal landscape of life. Life without art is unimaginable, almost painful to think about.

Growing up, there was not much in the way of paintings or such in our home, and I don't remember going to any museums until later in life. Somehow, I don't think my parents had a pastime of visiting galleries and museums while living in Palestine. I've never been there, but I imagine their everyday life in Ramallah, a land they loved, was pure art; the realism, the expressionism and the abstract.

Not growing up with proper museums and rooms of art does not mean that art can't find its way to you as you move through life.

As children, my dad would always draw with us. He was a natural calligrapher and artist. He could draw so many things: animals, trees, houses, and boats. I loved to draw with him. We did some creative 'art' projects growing up, and I enjoyed that so much.

As a mother and Tayta, I love being creative with the children. So much so, sometimes I forgot the child and lost myself in the project in my own childlike way. As a grown up, I love my watercolors and must find more time to paint. I also love ceramics and still have a few pieces I made in high school; one that took 1st Place in the county art exhibit.

I am so grateful that my children and my grandchildren love museums. I take such delight in the knowledge that they visit museums so regularly that they have an affinity and have established a respect and desire to witness art so early in their lives.

When I think about favorite artists and try to stitch together my "A" List , I get lost in the tapestry of this. If you ask me on a Monday following a magical weekend, I might think of a work of art or musician that is melancholy in tone to match my "it's Monday" mood. Bon Iver, Jeff Buckley, Innocence Mission, and Mazzy Star come to mind. Great artists like Andrew Wyeth or Vincent Van Gogh are Monday artists.

If you ask me on a Sunday morning, I suspect I would think of Walden or Satie. If you ask me when I'm doing the laundry, I may say Hopper or Norwegian Wood. Ask me when I am cooking, and I might say Georgia O'Keeffe or Cezanne. If I am thinking of the beloved Palestine and what my family lost, I think of Fairuz and more recently Jamal Badran, Chris Gazaleh and Tarik Kazaleh brothers from the San Francisco Bay Area.

Art is like an ingredient for a day well-lived. If you listen to your soul and follow its meanderings, you will hear whispers of your own senses which speak to you, and you can find the perfect images and sounds that are like fine finishing salts for your perfect day.

I think people call this mood music, or lighting, or maybe even mood art. Wouldn't it be grand to have a different piece of art that you could hang with a special meal that you have created? A piece of art that added flavor and texture to the dining experience you envisioned. Example? Gather the art, the ingredients, the linens, the plates, goblets and serve up a perfect Catalonian meal with *Basket of Bread* by Salvador Dali hanging on the dining room wall. This means nothing though without the art appreciators; like that saying, if a tree falls in the forest and no one is there to hear it, does it make a sound?

I wonder about such things because once the artist has

created something to behold, it's time for the witnessing. This interaction: the construct of the materials, the humanity that creates it, and the humanity that witnesses it is something the world needs - now more than ever.

Pablo Picasso once said that "the purpose of art is washing the dust of daily life off our souls."

Art connects us all, and it's not magic that people all over the world can have a similar experience looking at the same piece of art or listening to the same piece of music.

It mimics nature, and it nurtures our soul. In my home, I have several things from Palestine and a few things from my mother's and father's homes. These treasures, these works of art, bring me as close to the land where they were born as I think I could ever feel. The knowledge that they were made by hand in that distant land gives me great solace and hope, too, for future generations of artists in Palestine and throughout the world. It is the human experience of joy and of suffering that pushes the art out of the heart and into the world. Art heals us and transcends so much of the tragedy and despair of so many. It enlightens and gives us hope for humanity. It rests within us and resonates like a murmur or a bang.

Art I made with my granddaughters in the winter of 2023

RISE

Rise

A long time ago in my thirties, I read an article in Cosmopolitan magazine that said every woman should have a motto, and I knew what mine was without a second thought. Rise & Shine was my motto for sure. I'm quite sure if you asked my children, they'd quickly agree that it was Rise & Shine.

From as far back as I can remember, I've loved getting up early. There's just something about those quiet morning hours, before the world wakes up and starts bustling, that I crave. I feel such a deep sense of humility and appreciation for the fresh energy that fills our spirit every morning. I wake up renewed, ready for a new adventure and a brand new day.

I see each day as a fresh opportunity where we get to choose how we spend it. We are blessed to live in a world where this is true, though I know it's not so for everyone.

I am keenly aware that a spirit of joy and resilience lives in me and in my children. It has been passed as a treasured gift from our ancestors, and therefore I feel it is almost a requirement that I pay it forward too and spread that goodness, joy, and kindness—to splash it around here and there.

Every dawn is a chance to make a difference. It can be in the smallest way, or it can be extravagant and far-reaching. Depending on your vocation, personality, and abilities, you have the power to make great choices for your family, your community, and for yourself.

Rise and shine! If you think about it, that's exactly what this motto means: wake up each day and be a bright light, making the world better just by being alive. We only get this one life, and I say, live it fully and share your special gifts with those around you.

When I became a mother, I put this motto into motion. My children can tell stories about me walking into their rooms bright and early, opening the blinds, and cheerfully saying, "Rise & Shine" in my sing-song voice, which was probably annoying. Really, I don't think they minded it too much—except during their teenage years. Jameel, especially, was a late sleeper for a bit, so I learned to hold back the "Rise & Shine" melody when I knew he had been up late reading or hanging out with his friends. Elise, on the other hand, was always an early riser or maybe just protested less.

As adults, both of them wake up pretty early. With their beautiful families, they lead full lives and shine their way through their days. Of this I am certain.

I feel so blessed that they appreciate the simple pleasure of knowing what a new day holds. If I contributed to this in any way, it makes me incredibly happy, as it's been central to my life, and I can't imagine living any other way.

My dad used to tell me that I should have lived in the old country in the olden times, where everyone had to wake up early to attend to the chores of the day. I know this early bird path is not for everyone, but for me, it makes sense, so I go to bed eager for the renewal of sleep and for the new day that follows.

On the rarest occasion when I wake up past six o'clock, I feel like I've lost a big part of the day.

With this exaltation of the virtues of waking early, there is also something quite perfect when I stop to enjoy a lazy day. A day when you have no plans, and you can make it up as you go. When I was a child, of course, there were more of these. I had a few house cleaning and outdoor chores, as directed by our mom, but other than that, I could meander through the day. My lazy moments haven't changed much from since I was younger.

I loved to be outside, take walks in the park, looking at trees and flowers, trying to remember their botanical names. I almost always had my sketch pad with me. Sometimes I would draw; other times, I would jot down words that my experiences conjured up, and later I would write a poem. I was moved by Haiku in my early teens and then fell deep into a trance with Khalil Gibran and Rumi. Later, I was intrigued by Anne Sexton and intoxicated by the magnificent prose of Yates and Frost. I found that poetry was a way to articulate the inarticulate, and depending on my own reaction and interpretation, it either poured over me like sunshine or thundered above me like a storm.

I love poetry, although I don't read as much as I used to, reading poetry is still part of my lazy day. Other reading is part of most evenings, but reading on a lazy day puts it in a whole different perspective for me. Reading on a Sunday afternoon, for example, is such a splendid pastime. It usually results in the book slowly making its way to my lap as I drift off into a nap. Perfection.

Cooking is also a favorite pastime of mine on a lazy day—cooking for the sheer pleasure of it. A big pot of soup for the week, or organizing my spices, or making pickles.

I love to organize on any day, even a lazy day. For me, there's something uniquely comforting about being domestic, creating a serene and lovely space for oneself.

Sometimes, on a lazy day, I like to walk downtown and browse the shops. It's really relaxing when you're just browsing with no agenda.

I also love to call a family member or a friend to go for a walk or grab a cup of coffee. Having a nice, long visit is a great way to spend a lazy day. I still send note cards, too, and this is usually reserved for lazy days.

On Sundays, I like to take a nice bath, a luxurious long soak. Maybe a face mask or some other facial treatment. Sometimes I go for a manicure and pedicure and read. On a lazy day, I have been known to even stay in bed late. A day without an agenda is a great day to drive out to the coast. Nothing too novel, but worth noting that for me, a lazy day really means it's a just-about-me day, and I imagine that that holds true for most. A day for one to be with oneself and do as one wishes. I appreciate the luxury to have the freedom to do as I wish.

I don't think my mom and dad had so many of those lazy days, except maybe as they grew much older. We were definitely brought up to be busy and productive, but I think my sisters and I all figured out that 'me time' is essential and that being "lazy' as my mom might call it is just another way to say 'I'm busy at the moment'

I will have many lazy days as I grow older but while I live in this able body with energy to spare, I will always choose the Rise and Shine day. It will always take first place in the order of my life for as long as I am able. Energy is not endless, and I like to use it up every day. It is a gift that I feel blessed to open every morning and for this I am thankful and do not take it for granted.

Rise & Shine, people, the new day is upon us!

MENTOR

Mentor

I like to think that I have been a mentor to some.

For me, the word mentor holds grace, trust, and intention. It signifies that you have something of value to share. This awareness came to me when I became a parent. For me, that happened at a young age. In 1977, at twenty two I had my first child, and I met parenthood with ease and success. I was probably too young to have given it much thought, but I loved that singular purpose of motherhood. To love and to protect. It was natural and perfect in its simplicity.

In those earliest days of parenting, other young parents asked for my advice, and I gave it freely. Many of my cousins and friends from church were also young mothers. I think most parents reach out to each other about the challenges they face as new parents, but I was rarely the one asking questions, yet in turn, I was always being asked. I thought this was happening because I was relaxed and quite comfortable with all aspects of motherhood, and the moms that were asking me appeared a bit anxious about nursing or naptimes or any number of mom jobs. As time marched on and my children grew, the questions still came but were different with all the passing stages of parenting.

Watching my children raise their own children, along with their amazing partners, has been intensely satisfying. I can see so clearly that they carried with them the best parts of how they were parented and, along with their partners' contributions, designed wonderful parenting philosophies that are both nurturing and inspiring.

Later in my work life, I mentored many cooks who turned into chefs and was instrumental in guiding too many managers to count. If I tally up the number of people who've told me I've impacted their careers or lives, it is humbling, and I am proud of this. It feels right to help others on their journey whenever and however you can.

When you get to be 70 and have held leadership roles, you meet a lot of people that you can mentor and hopefully leave the world a better place in your own small way.

Engaging with people has been one of the most important and meaningful elements of my career. It has been incredibly rewarding to help others achieve their goals.

One of my longest stints has been with an independent retailer in the Bay Area, where close to 70 % of the employee population is Latino. I've been fortunate to work with remarkable people, most of whom were new to the country and the job and were extremely grateful for the support and guidance they received.

After nearly 24 years working with that retailer, many who started as dishwashers have risen to management roles. I think this has much to do with their brilliant and tenacious personalities and the power of their resilience. Much like my immigrant relatives, they made a place for themselves and excelled in whatever they set their minds to.

There are too many people to mention who came before those 24 years. Some coworkers, some friends, and some relatives. Over the years, I have received notes of gratitude, and I have held and cherished every single one.

On a more personal note, there is one person who consistently called me her hero, and that was my little sister, Michelle. She's eight years younger than me and I believe her when she says that she always looked up to me with adoration. It was precious; how much she loved me growing up, and she made sure I knew it. It has always been such an honor to be her big sister, and of course, I was also a big sister to Elizabeth and Sharon. This big sister role meant something to me, and I took it seriously.

Michelle was special, though, in the way she followed me around and wanted to do what I was doing. If I was choosing clothes to wear or giving myself a facial or a pedicure, she was there by my side and ready to participate. She was my shadow much in the way that I was dad's shadow when I was little.

She would leave me little gifts and handwritten love notes and ask for my opinion on everything.

I still have a beautiful old cigar box she converted into a love box, filled with all kinds of treasures. On the front, she drew and painted a scene of the two of us. When I got engaged to Jerry, she decorated the entry to our house with streamers and banners and insisted on giving me a manicure and pedicure. She picked the color, of course, and that was fine with me. She was, and still is, quite something with her amazing sense of humor and wily ways.

On my side of things, I've always looked after her in my own special way. She's a very gifted person who has had her fair share of trials that she overcame. I have a ton of respect for a person who can get back on their feet after life knocks them down.

I have wondered about mentors for me; who in my life was a mentor? Other than my parents, who should be mentors by nature, there was Aunt Azizeh, who showed me the meaning of joy in the kitchen. She also embodied how tough a woman could be. Her husband died at the doctor's office when she was about 40 years old, and she had many children that she then had to care for on her own. One day, my dad told me the story of how she was at her grocery store (that she ran after her husband died) and someone came to rob her. It goes something like his: she was sitting at the register reading a paper and eating her dinner, and the young man came in and pointed a gun right at her. Without hesitation, she reached over her paper, grabbed the gun, turned it on him, and he ran away! It's still hard to imagine anyone having the courage to do that. It was crazy and reckless, but I know she was NOT going to let that kid have the money she needed for her children. I loved her and always saw her as a warrior.

Another mentor was my friend Karen, who taught me to tap into the universe for inspiration and that taking risks was the point of life.

And dearest Siobain, who lives life to the fullest. She and I have shared so many abundant and magical adventures. Her heart is pure and filled with Irish humor, loyalty, and spirit.

And my Irish American John, who taught me how to trust, and that love could be unconditional in both directions. When I was in high school and studied a bit about Irish mythology and culture, I was smitten with all things Irish, and so it pleases me that my one true love, John, and my dearest friend Siobain are both Irish, and they love me fiercely, and I love them.

These are some of the people who taught me so many things, real things that helped me to be my best self.

And of course, my beautiful children. I look up to them in ways that surprise and overwhelm me at times. I can already see that I will feel the same about my grandchildren as I witness their incredible journeys.

Each generation is elevated to a higher place, brick upon brick, on the essence of the foundation that was placed before them by their parents and ancestors.

It's as though while we are here on Earth, one generation after the next, each of us building upon our sacred tower to the Heavens.

ROOMS

Rooms

The first bedroom I remember in detail was my bedroom on Terri Drive. I was five or almost five when we moved to that new house in the newly developed suburbs outside of Detroit. I have memories of rooms in homes that came before, but those memories are a blurry montage of various places we lived and most likely include the homes of relatives as well. We spent so much time visiting cousins that I am certain that all of those spaces melted together in my young brain to create the images I recall. There are several pictures I have seen of rooms we lived in and visited before our move out to the suburbs.

The bedroom I grew up in was unique because it had two doors; one that led to the kitchen and another to a central space that annexed all the bedrooms. I shared this space with my sisters, although which sister would vary as it changed often.

There was always movement and girl energy coming and going through that bedroom. Despite the frequent traffic through this room (thanks to those two doors making it a thoroughfare), I never seemed to mind. We loved running around the house in that loop, from the living room into the hallway, through our bedroom, into the kitchen, and back again. Every day and all the time. The house was filled with our laughter and the sound of my mom's voice yelling at us to stop.

I remember my bed, positioned against the wall to the kitchen. At night, I could press my ear against the cool surface and listen to the soft murmur of my parents' conversations. I discovered that the wall wasn't just a source of secrets but also great relief during hot summer nights. I'd press my back against it to stay cool while I quietly hummed myself back to sleep.

Sometimes, when I had a terrible dream about something bad happening to one of my parents or if I wet my bed or both, I would press my small body against the cool wall because I found it so soothing.

In the hallway outside our room, there were double louver doors that could close off the living room. After bedtime, when aunts and uncles were visiting, we'd sneak out of bed and stand behind those doors, peeking through the slats to catch glimpses of the adults while we listened to their conversations. Listening to them speak in their native tongue was in large part how I learned to speak Arabic. Sitting in that dark hallway behind those louvred doors, I felt like I was part of something secret, watching them laugh and converse, smoke cigarettes and drink coffee or Arak from Palestine.

I don't remember the colors or fabrics or many details of that first bedroom; what stands out most is the bed and chest of drawers, that cool wall, and the comforting sound of my parents' voices lulling me to sleep.

Sleeping was never easy for me as a child because I struggled with bedwetting, which caused nightly anxiety. But I made it through, as children do. Sometimes I was afraid to fall asleep, as I wondered where I would go when I fell asleep. This was a recurring question throughout my childhood and into my teems. I thought it was so strange to just not exist for several hours and couldn't reconcile the transition from awake to sleep and dreams and then back to awake.

I think night and the sleep it brings is the closest thing to death that we experience, and as a child, I didn't understand this concept or idea, but I felt it.

Nighttime brings us several hours of 'off' mode while we lie in our beds in our rooms. We just turn off, and the body goes into repair and rejuvenation for the next day. It's quite a miracle, really. The other thing I often thought about and still do almost nightly is all the people without a cozy bed in a warm room...and my prayers always included them.

As I got older, sleep came more easily for me. When I was around ten years old, my dad shared something revelatory with me when we were talking about how hard it was for me to fall asleep. He said falling asleep is just like flipping off the light switch for him, and I have been blessed with the same flip switch once I knew about it. Flip the switch and out I go. Something about this imagery was so helpful to me.

As an adult, I lay my head on the pillow, think about the day and things I am grateful for, things I could have done better, and then I flip that switch and I'm out.

Considering my history of bedwetting, I am grateful that I can fall asleep so easily. As a child, my bedwetting made nighttime pretty awful. This was part of my life until age twelve. From ten to twelve, it was not very often, but it was scarier as it became less frequent and caused much anxiety, never knowing when it would happen. It happened one last time a few days after my twelfth birthday. I tried so hard not to fall fully asleep so that I could catch myself if I needed to go to the bathroom. That finally ended, and to this day, when I hear about a child who struggles with bedwetting, my heart aches for them. It truly can define so much of your childhood experience. I rarely spent a night at a cousin's or friend's home for fear of the possibility that I would wet my/their bed. The other worst part of bedwetting was the shame and embarrassment I felt every time that my mother hung out the sheets and scolded me in front of others. I'm sure she was super frustrated and maybe she thought she could shame me into stopping. I know for sure that this strategy caused the bedwetting to continue longer due to the immense anxiety I felt every day.

But now; and maybe because of the intense gratitude I have for peaceful sleep, bedtime is the time for open windows, allowing the fresh air and fragrances of the night to wash over me as I drift off in the sanctuary of my room. I love this way of sleeping and think that the spirit can travel wherever it likes at night with the freedom of an open window. I don't fear death because I think it will be just like a long and lovely sleep.

I like to think that my children, grandchildren, and all those I love will be at peace with the knowledge of a loved one going off to the land of spirits and resting in peace.

That first room on Terri Drive taught me a lot about the night.

Later, I shared the middle bedroom in the hallway with my eldest sister, Noel. Each night we would lay our clothes out for the next school day. I have fond memories of that except for when we argued over wanting to wear the same clothes.

Another memorable room was on Ellen Drive in Livonia, which backed up onto that turkey farm. I can still hear the constant gobbling of the turkeys throughout the year, a sound that grew louder and louder until November, when Thanksgiving came, and then the sounds suddenly disappeared. After the harvest, it was eerily quiet, and we all knew why.

I was living in the rooms on Ellen Drive when the U.S.

astronauts landed on the moon. That night, after watching the moon landing, I went to bed in awe, after spending the evening staring up at the moon, trying to imagine what it must be like to stand on it and gaze back at Earth.

Looking back, I remember how often the beds and we sisters were shuffled around in various attempts by my mom to find the best sleeping arrangement for her five girls. It was like a never-ending camping trip, each night a new adventure.

I remember later rooms much more clearly, especially the bedroom on Six Mile Road. My parents, surprisingly, let me paint it in vibrant peacock green and naval orange, with mod fabrics that featured giant flowers in those same colors, plus white and yellow accents. To this day, I'm amazed they allowed me to go with such bold colors, but I must have been persuasive. That room felt like my own little world, a creative space where I could express myself. Having the freedom to paint that room was a major highlight of my life at the time.

Our family moved a lot, which meant I had many different bedrooms. One in particular on El Bonito when we first moved to Millbrae, California, was on an upper level with wraparound windows. The beds were positioned on a step-up platform, and the house had a mid-century deco vibe that I absolutely loved. The light in that room was incredible, flooding in through all those windows. I would sit on the bed and just stare out the window at the panoramic view for what felt like hours.

In May 2021, John and I visited Michigan. This was his first trip there, and with my mom, we showed him all our old homes and the park where we would play. It was a trip down memory lane, reconnecting with the places that shaped my childhood and all those many rooms that still hold so many memories. We had the best time, took lots of pictures, and stopped for lunch in Dearborn. I am so happy the three of us spent that day together driving around and telling stories. Those moments of remembering made my mom so happy at a time when she was starting to forget.

Terri Drive was our first stop, and it looked so small compared to what I remembered. The driveway seemed narrower, the garage where I spent so much time singing Maria from West Side Story was so much smaller, and our favorite front porch had changed. I saw the brick fireplace outside that had tiny "steps" that little feet could climb on. I used to climb up that brick exterior and sit upon a ledge that I think may have been intended for a planter. We used to play marbles against that brick façade. There was no more garden in the back of the garage. Dad nurtured that coveted space all the years we lived there, and it had turned into a junk pile.

I often think about the lovely gardens and the rooms in homes that mean so much to one family and how, after they move, that sanctuary that once was becomes something else entirely. It gives me a sad feeling and reminds me of the fleeting nature of our lives.

We also visited my dear father's resting place and all the aunts and uncles that rest under those trees alongside him in Parkview Cemetery in Livonia.

I think about the rooms of our lives and that in death maybe our spirits are free to roam and visit rooms and hallways and all the spaces we inhabited before.

Terri Drive

This is Ellen Drive where I ran outside (like everyone else) when we landed on the Moon in July 1969

six Mile Road

ESCROW

Escrow

Buy, buy, buy. My mother loved to buy things. I grew up feeling as though buying new things was high on the list of her favorite pastimes.

Confirming this, once after her 90th birthday, I asked her if she had any regrets, and she looked at me and said, ' I wish I didn't buy so many things'. I was quite shocked, really, never expecting her to say that so I asked her, "Why?" She said, "I could have done a lot of better things with all that money." I asked her, "Like what?

She said, 'more trips and nicer houses." That really made me laugh, but I would have to agree with her that trips hold great value, certainly more than stuff.

Saving was also an option that wasn't even on their radar, the way I remember. They certainly bought a lot of houses, maybe in search of the best one, and in her old age, it makes me chuckle that Mom still believed she could have had even nicer houses, even at 86, saying that she wanted to move to a nicer house.

Mom always loved the most expensive things. She especially loved handbags, beautiful bedding, linens and lingerie, clothes, shoes, and of course, jewelry and perfume. She really liked valuable items especially items that had coveted brand names.

Yes, she loved - almost worshipped a great trending name brand. I definitely did not follow her lead. I found her spending frivolous, impulsive, and sometimes I thought it was an act of defiance, for I believed then and still do that she felt that she should be able to have whatever she desired. She certainly worked hard and was deserving of so much. I think, too, that sometimes her spending was in retaliation for the money my dad spent on gambling. Two wrongs did not make things right, though, and they had some financial challenges because of these behaviors; the spending and the gambling.

When I think of expensive, I think of a home, a car, or a trip to a distant land. The first most expensive thing I ever bought on my own would definitely be my first house, which was $369,000. This was soon after my divorce from Paul Jordan. That marriage was the costliest event in my life, both financially and emotionally, for me and for my children.

After the worst, several years of my life, I finally moved out with Jameel to an apartment on Bayo Vista in San Rafael. Elise was already away at the University of Santa Cruz. That apartment had a little backyard area, a lovely Marin view, and a great pool. I used that pool almost every nice day after work. It was so comforting during those trying times. I took many walks around those hilly streets, taking in the views and fragrances. Life was starting to make some sense again. Jameel and Elise were my rocks and my reason for everything. We used to take drives to see Elise, and sometimes I would go solo, or she would come to us.

Two and a half years later, after some stability had set in and I had some money, I bought the house on Windsor Drive in San Rafael. I made this purchase on my own and felt so proud of this accomplishment after all I had come through. Finally, the worst was behind me.

Jameel lived there until he moved to Oakland a few years later, but I lived there for seventeen years and enjoyed my space and the surrounding neighborhood very much. I have so many memories of that home and all the wonderful gatherings we had there, along with the amazing walks I took in the neighborhood and on the ridge up above our hillside. Just above the open space behind my house, that beautiful ridge ran parallel to the majestic Mt. Tamalpais, stretching from north to south.

The house was built on a massive outcropping of granite and basalt. It is a wonder that anyone chose to build that house right there. My dad was fascinated by that; he thought the builder was crazy. I found it marvelous and quirky and always felt that house had a healing energy with all those giant rocks. The house had a view that was beyond description. Panoramic and facing the sunset, it was always a topic of conversation. The sky was so vast above the outline of Mt. Tam and the surrounding Marin hilly landscape that one could sit and marvel at it for hours. When my dad visited, you would always find him on the deck looking for any sign of wildlife or simply admiring the way I piled some stones one on top of the other.

I especially loved the night sky and watching the phases of the moon on its journey across the sky. This was a daily experience. Each early morning while it was still dark, as I walked from my bedroom to the kitchen to make my coffee, I would walk along a bank of windows with that moon in my sight and became so familiar with where it resided from day to day, week to week, the waxing and the waning, and some eclipses too.

The moon and her stars are what I miss most about that house. They were my companions.

A funny detail about that place was the runoff pipe on the opposite side of the driveway that I shared with a neighbor. When it rained, the water coming down the driveway sounded like a river. While it was lovely, it often discouraged people from walking or even driving up the driveway. For me, it was mostly wonderful because I loved waking up or falling asleep to the sound of that rushing water that made its way down the hillside through the runoffs that meandered down. Those run-off pipes were engineered and built from the top of the hillside, down and under the neighbor's house, and then exited on the long and wide driveway. When it was raining hard, I would go outside in my bare feet and walk down and back up the driveway just to feel the chilly water cascading across my feet and sometimes up to my shins.

My children had already known that neighborhood as they attended Sun Valley Elementary School when we first moved to San Rafael in '86. That school was just down the street from the home I ultimately bought in '99. Jameel's best friend at the time, Leo, lived right across the street from that school. I enjoyed walking around the neighborhood and on the trail behind the school to a different ridge.

Marin County is incredibly beautiful. The list of things I could say about it is endless. I especially loved the seasonal wildflowers during my walks and how they would change from week to week and sometimes day to day. Since my house backed up to open space, I could never keep much of a garden because the deer were always present. I used to joke that planting vegetables was like putting out a salad bar for the local animals.

I live in Walnut Creek now, and it too has beautiful outdoor spaces. John and I have found so many stunning trails and enjoy our home together so much. We have over 30 trees in our yard, which is kind of a full-time job, but they are worth it. I never realized how many shedding seasons trees have, and when you have many different species of trees, there is always something falling from them.

These areas that I love are in great danger due to drought, climate change, and the many fires. A few years back, Lake Tahoe was on fire, and the list is long of threatened environments close by and not so far away. Most recently, Los Angeles fell victim to fire fueled by the merciless Santa Ana winds.

I'm certain I'm not alone in asking the question: Should we stay in California? Whatever comes, whatever lies ahead, I am so grateful for the time I had in Marin County and for the purchase I made that day, standing on the deck and looking at the breathtaking view of Mount Tamalpais.

In honor of my father, Shawky Mousa, I've included a picture of that beautiful red fox that used to come and sit on the massive basalt and granite rock outside my front window. The fox visited often after my father passed. Dad would've loved this little creature and his foxy ways.

Red Fox in San Rafael on Our Windsor Rock.

HAWAII

Hawaii

If I could go to Hawaii every weekend, I would. There are so many places I love, but Hawaii is at the top of the list for many reasons. It's not such a long flight from my home in California, which makes it very easy to get there, but most importantly, it's beautiful beyond description. Hawaii is my paradise, or the closest thing so far.

Anyone who has been to Hawaii knows what I mean. It's like taking a dreamy walk through the most beautiful galleries of nature—majestic views, exotic wild colors, and the heady fragrances of blossoms and of sea and of sun and coconut oil kissed skin. The temperature is so ambient it feels like you could walk naked through the Hawaiian world and never need a thing. Even the rain is warm.

The scents and sights are so intense and amplified that they alert the senses. I feel fully awake every moment spent in the grandeur of the islands. And the fragrances aren't just floral; they carry hints of rain, greenery, skin, sky, herbs, wood, lū'au and happiness everywhere.

Hawaii is truly a feeling, a way of life, and a space in which to stand in wonder and awe of the natural world.

I don't think a person could truly be in Hawaii and appreciate its outstanding beauty without understanding the impact our immediate environment has on us. I've thought about people who live in places that are harsh, cold, dark, and gloomy, and how that must affect their energy and attitude. If we are one with nature, the natural energy surrounding us could indeed impact our mood.

We all know what it feels like to step outside into a beautiful summer day. This is a way of life in Hawaii. The people are friendly, the food is fresh and delicious, and the music is an elixir that brightens and satisfies the soul.

My first trip to Hawaii was in 1974 to the island of Oahu with Jerry for our honeymoon. I remember seeing those luscious, dark green crevice-gouged mountain sides for the first time and I was overwhelmed by their beauty. Everywhere I looked, beautiful and fragrant things jumped out at me. It's true that my exposure to anything like this up until that point consisted of Aruba, and while that had its own beauty, nothing compared to what I was experiencing in Hawaii.

Soon after we arrived, we took a bus ride to the opposite side of the island. At a bus stop, Jerry ran into one of his good friends from Torrance High School. He had moved to the island a few years prior and was at a small mall doing his laundry. This is where our bus stopped for a snack and a restroom break. Jerry and he literally ran into each other, turning the corner of the building. The next two days of our trip were spent going with him to a black sand beach that was only known to the locals, and while we were there, we ate enormous amounts of guacamole.

His friend always carried a little tin can of spices in one pocket and some limes in the other pocket. He would grab his Bowie knife, pick gigantic avocados the size of cantaloupes, and kneel down and make the guacamole, mixing it all together right in the avocado. The large fruit served as a bowl, too. I remember my sunburn from sitting on that beach too long, delirious from beauty and guacamole and delicious tortilla chips from his Jeep. At the time, all things avocado were amazing as avocados were unknown to me until we moved to California just two years earlier. But these Hawaiian avocados were something else entirely.

Other trips to Hawaii include watching surfing competitions at Pipeline, Rum tastings at plantations, early volcano visits, Sacred Falls, kalua pig roasting, so much swimming, hiking, frolicking and the best of times.

One magical night was spent watching Moana with John on a blanket under the stars on a big outdoor screen. My granddaughters, like so many, loved Moana, and I listened to the music with them countless times, I was in love with it too. Lying under the stars, thinking of them, and listening to the songs with the waves breaking close by was a wonderful experience that I shared with them later.

On a hike once in Kauai, John and I witnessed dozens of giant turtles laying their eggs on the sandy beach. We watched for so long, and skipped lunch altogether, for hunger did not visit us as we gazed in wonder.

One day was spent driving up to the volcano's edge, walking through orchid farms, then sailing at dusk holding onto my hat, sunglasses, and dress. John laughing with me while we were sailing alongside the sunset was unforgettable.

Some days we had too much Poki and Shave Ice because we couldn't get enough. We even loved the local Spam egg breakfasts. Everything tastes delicious in Hawaii, and it probably has much to do with the body in constant motion through the delights of the day.

Taking train rides through a local Zoo is an example of just how much adventure awaits every day. The beaches all beckon, and at night, the evening temperatures are so nice that we would sit out late every night and enjoy the perfect solitude and unique fragrance of the night.

These adventures happened in Jeeps, in kayaks, on sailboats but mostly on foot. Sometimes we hiked ten miles or more, but at least five to seven, just traversing and seeing as much as we could every day. The dashboard of our Jeeps always held a collection of flowers, shells, and random foraged treasures we picked up along the way. An altar of sorts, paying homage to our wildly wonderful Hawaiian adventures.

I write this with the deepest wish to return as soon as we can.

I hope to be there with my children and grandchildren one day.

The Kayak to Sacred Falls

OUTSIDER

Outsider

I never went to prom, and I didn't want to at the time, but a person doesn't know what they don't know, and looking back knowing what I know now, I'm sure I missed out. My parents were strict, and sometimes it was easier and felt better too, for me to say I didn't want to go rather than hear them tell me I couldn't go.

As I matured, I came to realize that I could have fought for some of those milestones in high school and in life. Looking back, I still believe that if a person is not aware that they have a choice, then they may not venture to make one.

It is true, though, that in the end, and for a variety of reasons, I wasn't too interested in the social aspects of school. I can clearly recall feeling separate and different from my classmates and teachers, and I know that influenced my attitude.

One high school highlight was helping my best friend, Karen, get ready for her prom. I remember feeling genuinely happy for her as we were putting on her makeup and doing her hair, and also relieved that I wasn't going. Anyone who has ever felt like an outsider might be able to relate. For much of my elementary and middle school experiences, I floated my way through and mostly circumvented the social moments that I wasn't unable to avoid altogether. I was acutely aware of how different my family and I were, and that getting too close to anyone at school would sometimes result in an awkward situation for me, or so it seemed.

What I most feared was that they would invite me over or ask if they could come over. At that time, I felt uncomfortable with the entire prospect of either of those possibilities. I was enormously proud of our culture and traditions but did not feel that my mom or dad would have been truly supportive; whether this is true or not, it was how it seemed to me, so I rarely asked.

When it came to Karen, I did go to her home often, and she was over a lot too. This was enough for me. Karen and her family loved our food, our music, and our traditions. Looking back, I am certain that most people would have loved it all too. Karen ingratiated her way into our lives, and my parents liked her right away. My mom had met her mom at the market, and they chatted about their daughters and their silly ways. Momma never told me that, but Karen's mom did. By that time, Mom had been in America for close to 17 years and had become much more outgoing. She was more accepting, and I think that sometimes my sisters and I took advantage of that where we could.

My sister Sharon was our rebel, and I am quite sure she felt like an outsider, too. Sharon gravitated towards things and people that would most likely cause her to get in trouble, which I remember her doing as often as she could. She was the opposite kind of outsider; the rebel outsider, and I was the fearful outsider. She was fearless and impulsive, and these attributes allowed her to experience what I refer to as a normal teenage journey. I remember her as a child sitting on the front lawn at Terri Drive with her hair wild and her face hot red with anger and defiance because Mom was calling her in, and she was not planning to move a muscle.

I wish I had thought to relieve her (as if that were possible) of some of that rebellion and try it out for myself. Now, I'm not saying that I always did exactly as I was told, but I surely could have spoken up more.

Each of us girls has two to three years between us, and a

couple of years can make all the difference in that first-generation world we were experiencing with our parents. When we sisters speak of these things, each of our perspectives and perceptions are wildly different. Of course, each of us daughters had our own unique experiences growing up and living a first-generation childhood and adolescence. In fact, I'm fairly certain that each one of my sisters will scratch their heads and think " I don't remember that" or have any number of questioning thoughts when they read my memoirs. That is just the way it is when you have siblings all living together with the same people but with varying experiences and the memories of them. We were all in the same boat but that didn't mean we were all heading in the same direction.

When your parents are navigating and growing accustomed to a new way of life, things change dramatically from one daughter to the next in line. They became more open to our exposure to the American ways and more at ease.

The feeling of otherness and not truly feeling like you belong was amplified when the news was filled with stories of Yasser Arafat and the PLO (Palestinian Liberation Organization) and my parents worried that we could be targeted. I remember my mom telling someone we were Lebanese. When I asked her about that, she said it was better to say that and keep us safe. In those days, we were outsiders living our new life in America and holding closely the Palestine my parents and sister left behind.

In my adult life, I came to learn that I was never really an outsider and recognized that I had so much more to offer the world. This was exquisitely liberating, and I taught myself and my children to share their beautiful culture as often and as proudly as possible.

This paradigm shift was substantial for me in my own

way and in my own time, and I finally understood that the joy, comfort, and deep pride I felt for my culture must be shared in every aspect of my life. Keeping it to myself was never going to be okay again.

And through this experience, I grew to feel a kind of sadness for people who didn't have the richness of a strong heritage and traditions to illuminate their lives.

I cherish our Palestinian heritage and feel so blessed because of it. When I can share any part of it, I do. Like all other cultures and traditions, mine is a gift to the world.

TRAVEL

Travel

As a child, as far back as I can remember, and until I was about thirteen, I had the same dream most every night. With arms outstretched like wings and my feet bare, I was flying over emerald, green hills, swooping down to precarious lows and soaring upwards to the bluest of heights. The dream was always filled with color, wonder, and glee. There were moments of fear, too, because in every dream, I almost crashed into one of the green hillsides, but as I was about to crash, I would wake up. I never woke up feeling scared, as I was still enveloped in the vibrant colors and vistas that had just surrounded me.

I believe that this repetitive dream inspired my desire to travel. In my teens, I began to imagine all the places I would go. At the park, with my sketch book in hand, I would draw imaginary places that were filled with desirable images and sometimes I would make up an imaginary name for the place I created.

When it comes to travel, I have been extremely fortunate because my profession afforded me many trips to Europe. I have traveled dozens of times to France, Spain, Greece, and Italy. Less frequent trips to so many other places, but the European 'food" trips were often and quite unique. Within these countries, I have crisscrossed the well-known and lesser-known regions and visited farmsteads, artisanal shops, and producers' homes. Visiting the homes of artisan producers has always been the highlight of these trips.

These adventures were remarkable, and I was always aware of just how lucky I was to participate. Indeed, I felt both honored and grateful for these experiences and for the beautiful memories I hold of the families I met and the amazing foods they lovingly crafted and placed before us to enjoy.

Many of their products traversed continents and found themselves on kitchen tables so far from their origins. I wonder how often most people stop to consider where the food they eat comes from and what it took to produce. How many generations of a family have made the same cheese or olive oil, vinegar, wine, or biscuits? For me, it's a staggering and beautiful thing to consider. I like to share these considerations with others and do as often as I can while we enjoy a bite of this or that.

The same is true for all of the beautiful local products we consume daily. Thinking of the hands that were involved in the production of any food, or the growing of any produce offers additional benefits to the pleasure and the bodies experience while enjoying it.

I have collected an unknown number of photos of these trips. Pictures filled with the faces and hands of the people who make or grow these artisan foods. Pictures of the vast number of places that we would trek to many times, so far from everything. Some of the places were almost surreal as we walked, witnessed, and finally tasted. The vistas, aromas, flavors, and sounds of the people and their work created the most exquisite sensory journey. When I think about these trips, I hold my hand to my heart and take a moment to acknowledge how truly fortunate I have been to enjoy these life-altering experiences.

Most of the people I met on these visits had never left their village. They had never traveled *anywhere*. They do what they do for their whole lives, and that is that. They live and die on their land. They love, work hard, and raise their families together until the torch gets passed. And when it gets passed, the next generation already knows exactly what to do. The work and the foods they produce require generational oversight and passion.

On one of these extended trips traveling across the entire country of France, from North to South and then West to East, my clothes went to Russia instead of with me to France, and I hardly noticed because quite frankly, from moment to moment my heart and mind were filled up with so much more than whatever clothes I had packed. I stopped at a local store off the Autobahn to pick up an extra set of shorts and a couple of t-shirts, and I was good to go. I really needed nothing more than the clothes on my back and my experience of each day. I washed my socks and undergarments at the end of each day and hung them to dry on my balcony for the night. There was more than one occasion when they were still damp when I left for the day's excursion.

A favorite trip was when I visited Crete. I had the deepest yearning to be on my ancestral land, and I was so close, in fact, that it was the closest I had ever been to my family's beloved Palestine. I could feel the proximity as I experienced the similarities in food, people, and traditions. Even the Greek Orthodox churches on the hill fueled the fire in my heart with a deeper longing to know the land of my parents.

My son Jameel made that trip to Palestine years ago, and for this, I am eternally grateful. I hope that I will travel there too.

When I was on the island of Crete, I planted an olive tree. The olive oil in Crete is incredible with its dark green, sharp, peppery flavor. When it is just pressed, it is unforgettable and reminds me so much of olive oil from Palestine. I can still smell the air and the olive groves of Crete and feel the dirt between my toes. Sometimes, I like to garden without shoes, so I took them off when I was planting that tree.

The colleagues I was with had a good laugh and took a photograph of me in my bare feet standing by my olive tree. A couple of years ago, one of them sent me a picture of that beautiful tree that is now 24 years old and produces beautiful, perfect olives. How I wish I could get some of those olives to cure & brine.

From that hillside, the sea was visible, and I remember looking as far as I could and thinking ...just over there is where my mom left her family and where my dad left his.

I stood there and cried and felt as though the tears that flowed were my parents' tears and that maybe there was someone on a hillside across the sea crying for the ones that had left home never to return again. As I returned to my group in the olive grove, there was much laughter and an anticipation for the meal that was being put before us. So many small dishes of mezze, much like my Palestinian brothers and sisters just across the sea enjoyed.

Travel allows a person to be fully engaged, away from their everyday routines. It can offer an awakening of the senses, a fulfillment within you that can be both invigorating and inspiring. For this, I intend to travel as much as I can for as long as I live.

The things I witness while traveling breathe clarity into my human experience. I took two trips last year for my 70th birthday. Oaxaca was the first trip, and this was with my entire family. Elise was almost seven months pregnant with baby Khalil, and so he was there too!

We went to Oaxaca during their Semana Santa (Easter Week), and it was perfectly delightful in every way. The trip was more than I could have ever hoped for, and I am certain that my children and grandchildren will remember it with fondness forever. It was deeply satisfying, and I treasure each memory as sacred.

The second 70th celebration was in Ireland, where we stayed with our dear friend Siobain at her beautiful farmhouse near Ennis in County Clare. Her sister Shirley and brother in law Duncan were there too. They are all so much fun and absolutely a joy to be with! There we explored the Wild Atlantic Way of the Connemara Coast. Siobain planned the most magical trip and upon our arrival presented me with the itinerary. She is always filled with so much magic and so many surprises! This itinerary included oyster and abalone tastings, a sea kelp trek on the shore and a follow up menu tasting of various and glorious dishes made with the offerings of the sea. This delightful tasting took place while sitting in a three wall make shift but perfect "dining room" facing the sea. The itinerary included a castle stay, whisky tasting, birthday cake overlooking the sea, magical meals at her home, and rainy walkabouts. I mustn't forget the sauna and ice cold shower that us three girls had on the lakeshore below the castle. What fun! And upon our return to the castle, they came with me to my room and when we opened the door, John had decorated the entire room with every manner of Happy 70th Birthday decorations and balloons that Siobain had brought with her. They had a plan to surprise me with this, and it certainly worked. I was delighted mostly by their coordination and love...

I can never capture the feeling of being in Ireland; this was my second trip, and I fully expect to be there again soon.

I think that my life would be much less full if I had never traveled. Each trip has added a layer of pleasure and knowledge my journey; each a page in a chapter of which I hope there are many still to unfold, and yet if my days on earth are done tomorrow, I feel fulfilled.

Travel is so important and often I have wished that schools would include travel in their curriculum. If children could experience different cultures, traditions, and see people who look or live differently than they do, the seeds of acceptance can be planted and nurtured. Exposure is everything, and travel makes this possible.

I wonder what my dad and mom thought on those first days they walked into America, into a life and landscape so foreign to them. I know it must have been awkward and terrifying, yet surely, there was some excitement too for everything that would come after.

Dingle, Ireland

Bra, Italy

Jameel sitting in his kitchen in Brooklyn.

MOTHERHOOD

Motherhood

I believe that Motherhood is the most divine realm in the universe where the power of love and light ignites all other places. The purity of a mother's love is unparalleled; it is an unwavering bond between humans and one that I have been so grateful to experience.

On that extraordinary day that I became a mother, the strangest experience of my life occurred right after the birth of my daughter, Elise.

To begin with, giving birth is an intense act of faith that everything will be as it should, and that the whole affair will be filled with joy. These things held true for me, and it was also unforgettable for more reasons than one might imagine.

My precious and beautiful daughter, Elise, was born with much difficulty as I had pre-eclampsia in my third trimester.

I spent several days in the hospital during those final weeks before giving birth because of this condition which even today is quite serious and needs to be monitored closely.

During my last weeks, everything seemed to be under control, but when it was time to go to the hospital for delivery, things started going sideways as my blood pressure was very elevated, and medications and IV's started being administered. The doctors and the nurses were trying to control my blood pressure and my contractions at the same time. No easy task.

The hours of labor passed so slowly, and I kept thinking about my poor little baby and how hard all of this must be for her. I worked hard to stay as calm and as focused as possible, thinking that this would soothe my baby still inside my womb. After over 30 hours of labor, Elise was born, and I saw her for only a moment before they whisked her away. I was euphoric holding her in the warmest of embraces… but then they took her away abruptly to check on her and do all the "new baby things and run tests."

She looked perfect, so things seemed to be ok, although I knew that I did not feel quite right. What did I know about how a new mother is supposed to feel post-delivery? I took comfort in the doctor telling me that I just had a difficult labor, but that I was fine now, and everything was going to be ok. And then he left.

Within moments, things took an unbelievably bad turn, and what happened next changed me forever. My blood pressure plummeted, and I remember feeling something terrible was happening to me and that I had to get the remaining nurse's attention quickly.

It felt as though ice water was oozing through my veins and out through my pores.

Jerry was there, and a nurse was still in the room cleaning up. It felt as though it took me several minutes to push just two words from between my lips ..S o m e t h i n g's …w r o n g…..and almost immediately there was a code blue alarm and the last thing I remember in that moment was the sound of my poor mother screaming in the hallway.

Then there was a strange nothingness for a moment… until I saw my doctor rush back into the room, and I saw the code cart was there. I don't remember anything about the cart or paddles when they were used to try and revive me. What I do remember is that suddenly I was sitting upright in an old school chair with bright red enamel legs and one of those flip-down desk tops. I was sitting there smiling, and what felt like soft laughter was coming from my lips while wondering what all the fuss was about. I looked down at myself and at the red enamel legs and felt incredible peace and what felt to me like joy.

From that chair, I watched the doctor run back into the room and because he understood exactly what needed to happen, he flew into action. He knew that my condition and the medication I had during labor could cause my uterus to flip, leading to internal hemorrhaging. Without going into too much detail, the excess blood was pressing on my organs, causing a dire situation.

Thank God he was still in the building when he, in his suit and tie, ran back into the room, took off his jacket, put on one glove on his right hand, and reached into my body to pull down the uterus. I was watching all of this from my school chair and as he did that I could see the river of blood pouring into the basin below me at the end of the table I had been lying on. There was a big round mirror above me during the delivery, so I was able to witness the birth, and from behind my body that was lying lifeless on that delivery table, I was able to see the doctor's work in the reflection of that mirror.

I was unafraid and simply fascinated watching all of this from behind the table, floating in my red school chair.

I remember looking at myself lying on the table, thinking I looked so peaceful. I watched the blood pour out with no fear—just peace. I don't remember exactly when, but somewhere around the moment of watching the blood hit the basin, I was back in my body – in an instant, and that was it. My spirit found its way back to me.

The next day, I was telling my doctor what happened, and it was very awkward and strange then trying to tell the story, and it still is to this day; and even in this moment I still feel a little strange when I share this experience.

At that time, it felt like a dream. I didn't recognize it as an out-of-body or near-death experience (*NDE*) until Dr. K told me that the chair with the red enamel legs was, in fact, directly behind the head of the delivery table.

That school chair was in the room, and I had never seen it before!

That's where my spirit or consciousness traveled during the post-delivery trauma, as though I just took the closest seat and sat there waiting for them to fix me, knowing everything would be ok.

Once I knew about the chair, and the doctor explained that he believed "sometimes people have near-death experiences and leave their bodies," I knew that's what had happened to me.

The very next day, Dr. K was slated to be on the talk show "Not for Women Only" on a local channel. He called the nurse and asked her to come to my room and tell me that he was going to talk about me on the show. She turned on the TV, and I watched as he talked about the power of motherhood and shared the experience he had just had with me the day before. He explained how, even though I could have been pronounced clinically dead, I did not die because I knew I had a new child to care for. He continued, saying that the survival rate in near-death experiences is highest for new mothers because the innate nurturing response and faith of a mother for her newborn is unmatched. Listening to him that day is when it really hit me—what had happened.

I felt blessed for many reasons: for the beautiful child I had just delivered to the world, for my wonderful family, for my brilliant doctor, and for all the people who took care of me. And for that red chair that held me so safely until it was safe for me to return to my body.

This experience was wildly strange and caused discomfort for most when I shared it. It is also indelible in my mind. I remember it often, and I know it has shaped how I see the world as a mother, as a daughter, a sister, and with John. It has woven itself around me and into every aspect of my life. When I look in the mirror and see my living and breathing self look back at me, I am awestruck and energized by the gratitude for my life and also for the keen awareness of the fragility of life.

Indeed, each of us will be dust in the wind, and the winds of death come for all of us. Since that experience, I have been able to tap into something much greater than me, a deep unknown in the universe that whispers to me. Through that near-death experience, I have found a deep sense of peace and love. I do not fear death; in fact, when I have been in a room with someone who is close to death, I feel as though they see me as a conduit that allows them easy passage. This has happened three times. Each time, a great peace washed over me, as they passed, as though I felt their soul move into the next life, and it is impossible to explain beyond that.

My heightened sixth sense seems to awaken most around my children, grandchildren, and others I love deeply. Motherhood and this sixth sense are happy partners. This sense informs me about my loved ones; from simple arrival times after a trip (as though an alarm goes off that says Elise is home now, or Jameel just landed) to more complex thoughts and feelings about meaningful experiences and conversations.

There is much written about life after an NDE, and I have

explored this phenomenon. It added extra layers of empathy and gratitude to my journey through motherhood and for the rest of my life from that one transformative experience.

Under normal circumstances, becoming a mother changes one forever, and in some more unexpected circumstances, it does as well. That day, I breathed a second first breath. Years later, loving my children I understood that I survived not to live but to begin again as a mother.

Elise Noel Harb – Born in San Francisco on April 22,1977

GRANDPARENTS

Grandparents

My children, Elise, and Jameel, were wildly lucky to have all four of their grandparents in their lives until they were both over thirty.

I have often wondered how often this happens and came to believe it to be highly unusual. I have never verified its rarity, but I have never known anyone else who can say this. Not only were their grandparents alive, but most importantly, they interacted with them on a regular basis. I am clear-eyed in knowing that this has been such a blessing in their lives. Rizik & Jean Harb and Shawky & Jannette Mousa. Of these beautiful ones, only Jannette and Jean are still alive and Elise and Jameel are both well into their forties now.

When I think about my children and the incredible people they have turned out to be, I know some of this can be attributed to the exceptional gift they were afforded by having all of their grandparents in their lives until their thirties.

The legacy of their ancestors, not through word of mouth, not by reading a story, but by actually living their lives alongside them; is priceless. My children will surely tell stories of their grandparents to future generations, and I hope that my role as a grandmother will last for many years to come where I continue to share with each of them my unique influences and style of life, love, and play. I hope that these beautiful humans will cherish my stories and be the new keepers of family and tradition as they move through their own journeys.

I am blessed with Audriana, 11, Amina, 10, Alma, 3, and Khalil, now 11 months, and hope my future days with them are abundant and filled with stories and with song.

My love for them is beyond words. It's beyond the beyond of what I know. It's the same love I feel for my children but then exponentially expanded by the love they have for their own children which I witness with joy. This kind of compounded love is of divine origin, and the moments spent together are pure and golden.

I have always hoped that my grandchildren see me; their "Tayta" as a place; an island of laughter and trust and unconditional everything. It is such an honor to be that older and extra parent.

Grandparents can make all the difference in the lives of their grandchildren and their parents. This profound resource should never be underestimated. When I think about my children and the incredible humans they are, I know that being raised by six 'parents' gave fullness to all aspects of their lives and ultimate personalities.

To ponder the complexity and magnitude of the influences of the parents, but also the two sets of grandparents sheds light on the teachings and experiences acquired growing up in this magical way.

Six parents in each of their corners rooting them on while watching over them and guiding them forward.

Add to this the abundance of heritage; in part their Palestinian ancestry and traditions; not just through word of mouth and stories but through the living legacy they shared together as they stood alongside their Tatas and Seedos and walked together through life.

My children will tell stories to their children and their grandchildren. And on it goes. I know that this pathway to our culture will narrow with each generation, but for now, I do my share and it is enough and fills me with the deepest satisfaction. In their honor, I am devoted to the storytelling as it is a way to return the favor of the grandparents before me, for their love and devotion.

I had a relationship with only one of my grandparents. The others either died before I was born or lived in Ramallah, so I never got to meet them. From Heaven or from Ramallah, I am certain they still watched over us. That's what grandparents do.

I am incredibly grateful for the grandmother that I knew here on Earth. She taught me many things. Zarifeh Mousa lived with us on and off from the time I was little. The majority of the Arabic I learned was a result of her being in our home, as she did not speak English.

She was a simple woman, and in many ways, I loved her for that, and she always reminded me of my dad.

Living a simple life in harmony with nature is something that, for me, was the essence of who she was. I liked this about her, and it left a mark on me.

Some treasured memories come to mind. On many occasions, we would crack walnuts together. Of course, a person can buy walnuts that are already shelled, but the idea here was that we would pay half the amount for them and have fun visiting and cracking them together. Naturally, we ate plenty while we cracked away. I still love to crack walnuts, and I can't do it without thinking of her.

She praised me regularly because I loved to clean and do kitchen work, and of course, these things generated worthy praise for a young Palestinian American girl. After all, the one true and constant plan was that we would marry, have children, and take care of our families and homes.

And this held true, even though I've worked for 99% of my adult life. As much as I enjoy working and being self-sufficient, the joy of creating a beautiful, aesthetically pleasing, and serene sanctuary that fosters good health, and well-being is essential to my life.

I like to think of my grandchildren being in my home and feeling a beautiful energy that inspires them and brings them joy. This makes sense to me and brings me a deep happiness.

Another wonderful memory I have of my grandmother is helping her with her bath. She always wanted me to scrub her back and help her braid her hair after washing it. My other sisters did this too. I felt so honored to help her bathe, after all, she was a most special person in my life. I was young and didn't fully understand that she wouldn't be around forever, so looking back I am happy that I did this as often as I could. I felt a deep sense of pride and tradition when I helped her with these things and expected it to always be that way…

It would have been wonderful to know my other grandparents. I can only look at photos and listen to stories, imagining what our interactions would have been like. I always wished that my parents told me stories about their parents, but it was a rare occurrence especially from my mom. My father died before my grandchildren were born so I tell them stories of my father and of my grandmother. I recently found a recording that I want to play for them so they can hear his voice.

Knowing who came before us and understanding their identities and personalities as much as possible helps us learn more about ourselves. I know that Elise and Jameel's strong sense of self is a testament to this way of thinking. It's a bit like looking in a mirror and seeing beyond the face in front of you into the past lives, the trials and tribulations, the joys and sorrows, and the deepest kind of love.

A love that passes from one generation to the next and from one home to the next, where you will always find a bowl of walnuts.

TRADITION

Tradition

Growing up in a Palestinian American family came with a universe filled with traditions.

Almost every tradition centered around family and food. And of course, for every *hafla* or party, you had to prepare food. And preparing the food meant the women gathered and joined forces to create numerous beautiful traditional dishes. It was the mezzeh, the main courses, and of course, the honey, nut, date, or cheese-laden desserts.

Some gatherings were less elaborate than others, like the family picnics. These were especially fun. We listened to Arabic music, and the men played cards; we called it *shadeh*. There were always so many cousins around, so there was never any shortage of playmates.

One of my favorite traditions was going to the farms to pick whatever was in season. We would go with my mom and some of my aunts, and then we would come to our house or to one of their homes to prepare whatever vegetables or fruit we picked.

It was quite the collaboration, and at the end, when the work was completed, each person would take their share home to their families. This was a lot of fun for the youngsters because the moms were busy working and gossiping, and the kids could pretty much do whatever they wanted.

There were so many other traditions that it is impossible to name them all.

Here are a few...

1) When a new baby comes to your house for the first time, you must gift them with a precious metal

2) You must always kiss the elders hello and goodbye - on both cheeks

3) When someone visits, you must serve them food and drink

4) Having shai in the evening

5) Zait and Zaatar for breakfast with olives, tomatoes, and labna

6) Gifts, gifts, gifts… giving gifts whenever possible

7) Shopping for bargains and announcing to extended family what you paid

8) Negotiating the best price wherever possible

9) Giving the elder the passenger seat in the car or the best seat in the room

10) Overdressing children when it's chilly

11) Wearing all of our gold jewelry and passing it down to daughters and daughters-in-law and then to granddaughters

12) Coloring our Easter eggs with onion skins

13) The uncle on the mom's side is going to the bride's home before the wedding to escort her to the church

14) Staying in touch with all the elders

15) All the women going to grave site at the break of dawn the day after the burial and taking kahwa Arabia for the deceased

16) Storytelling

17) Making mamoul for weddings

I love all of our Palestinian traditions, even the less desirable gossipy ones, and feel blessed to be part of this amazing culture. I cannot imagine how different my life would be without the beautiful textures and flavors of a Palestinian American childhood.

The love and support that I felt every day could at times be overwhelming, but I would not trade it for anything.

My children, too, are blessed to take part in the amazing history they have inherited. Their traditions will be their own, but they will include many of the same ones I was able to experience, of this I am certain, as I witness it daily.

I think about the tradition of the American holiday Thanksgiving. Even though I cringe at the knowledge that this holiday was borne of oppression and bloodshed of the Indigenous peoples, it has become a family tradition of gathering and feasting. As I grew older, I became increasingly aware of the relationship of the real story behind "Thanksgiving" and its relationship to my own people's story. And still, we celebrate the giving of thanks, and for me and my family, this harvest holiday is a way to bless and commemorate all that came before, of their trials and their sufferings and their joys. We would fill the house with American and Palestinian dishes, and my father and I would carve the turkey while my mom presented the many dishes.

For me, this singular day of feasting bears witness to the past, for the best of what life can offer us and all that was taken away.

As we light the candles at the dinner table, I think of the heartache and the joy, and of the hope that rises.

After my father died, we had one last Thanksgiving together in Michigan. We set Dad's place at the head of the table. While we sat quietly before the meal started, I remembered how daddy looked the prior Thanksgiving as he set eyes on each one of us around the table. I will never forget that moment as though he knew it was his last Thanksgiving with us. But every holiday since, it is my dad I visit with as I sip my morning coffee.

He is always right here with me, and I will never carve a Turkey (or any cut of meat for that matter) without thinking of him.

Shawky Jamil Mousa 1931-2012

A gift from my mother for my 50th birthday

Mom, Audriana, and Amina making Mamool

Some Of Our foods In Our Pottery

MEZZEH

Mezzeh

I have always loved to taste different types of foods together.

In our culture, we have a thing called Mezzeh, which is the Arabic word for appetizers. Mezzeh consists of many different foods, cheeses, dips, olives, breads, pickled vegetables, roasted nuts, and sometimes succulent lamb football-shaped kiftas or other heartier foods like lamb or spinach pies.

Mezzeh is a perfect way to sample the utterly delicious and distinctive flavors of Palestinian cuisine.

Olives are the centerpiece for me. I love the green tart and sour, fresh-made olives that my mom made. They are one of my favorite things. Everything else that goes on the table is a perfect complement to the olives.

Our mezzeh is a meal for most people, but only the first course, the whetting of the appetite for us.

Mezzeh, appetizers, starters, bites, and grazing boards have become a common practice in the American lifestyle. I have many friends who eat like this every day, too, making a meal out of all the small plates.

Each of the elders in my family would serve many of the same dishes of Mezzeh, but Aunt Nuha, upon our arrival in California, elevated Mezzeh to new heights for me. The dishes of Mezzeh that streamed from her small kitchen were endless. There were some dishes that I had not seen before, and I tried everything. This "first course" lasted a couple of hours, with the brothers newly united. Mousa, Nabil, Shawky, and Fuad, all so happy to be together again, sitting around the table holding their glass of Arak while they laughed, talked, and enjoyed all the wonderful foods with their piece of khubiz in hand, dipping up the next bite.

One of my favorite outcomes of eating this way is that it leads to new combinations of flavors in one bite. Having mezzeh definitely creates an environment where a person can become very adventurous with their food.

I have always loved trying different bites of food together. Sometimes we have dried fruits, and I would mix them with a nut and a cheese, which I always thought was such a natural combination, and it turns out that's what you see on today's modern cheese boards.

Eating in this way, a bite of this, a bite of that, became my food ideal. It is almost impossible for me to eat any meal without wanting to explore how two unlikely foods might taste together. This is how I cook as well. Ask my children, and they will tell you that unless the dish I make is Palestinian, the meal is always a new creation. They learned at an early age that meatloaf or tuna casserole or other 'American" inventions would never taste the same twice because I make these dishes with whatever I have on hand and whichever the winds of creativity are blowing when I am in the kitchen.

One thing I always loved was dessert with cheese, for example, any slice of pie is great with some kind of cheese or ice cream. I'm sure this love of cheese for dessert came from our beloved *knafeh,* that divine cheese and shredded dough dessert we grew up with. Other fun combinations: I like to mix peanut butter in my oatmeal or any hot cereal. Speaking of peanut butter, I always made sundaes of layered ice cream with peanut butter chocolate, bananas, and ice cream for my children when they were small. That was always a special treat. Most of us already know that peanut butter is good with so many things.

I say you never know how delicious foods are together unless you try them. Certainly, peanut butter with bananas and chocolate and ice cream is not novel, but the sublime collection of these different ingredients sends a signal to the brain that some foods are better together than they are on their own.

Endless possibilities, yes…but not meant for the ones out there that don't want their food to touch the plate.

For those, I say start with an olive and see what happens. I'm fairly sure you will have a piece of cheese next, and if you don't want them to touch, guess what - they are touching in your mouth.

Mezzeh is at the beginning of every delicious journey. It has a specific pacing, a sense of ritual that encourages us to stop, look around us and take in the beauty of our loved ones, the beauty of the dishes and this particular moment in time and to hold it close until the next gathering.

Mezzeh is rooted in the land. Olive oil, za'atar, chickpeas, yogurt balls, lemon, garlic, sumac. The plates are all in the center of the table using bread instead of utensils. Conversation is part of the mezzeh. Mezzeh carries memory and identity, it reflects village life and seasonality. It resonates resilience, making richness from modest foods and generosity even when ingredients may be scarce. It is much more than food.

SIMPLICITY

Simplicity

When I look closely, the world around me is immensely different from what it was when I was a child.

With the advent of social media and the expansion of commerce, the planet seems much smaller, because everything the world has to offer has become easily accessible with a swipe of your finger.

There are certainly some benefits, numerous ones for which I am grateful. Mostly for me and others who have loved ones far away, social media provides much comfort through connectivity. I will take a virtual visit from my son and his beautiful family every chance I get. Even with little Alma and Khalil, just across the bay. A simple meaningful connection makes my day.

This is wildly different than the olden days, where, for example, my mother never saw her mother's face again, once she left Ramallah. No social media then, and it is painful to imagine living that way now, unable to easily connect with your loved ones.

As an elixir, on many days, I find myself thinking about how most things in life are still the same. It's the simplest of things; a walk in the park is still a walk in the park. A dinner with a friend is still a cherished pastime. Getting together with family is better than anything, and I fully believe that these simple things will hold great value forever. There are so many wonderful possibilities that can take place right where you stand. The simplicity of helping someone in need or stopping to gaze at the moon. These things feeds the soul. These things are constant throughout human history and undeniably at the heart of everything.

No amount of screen time or scrolling will ever replace these things.

Being out in nature is the mandatory transaction in the human experience. I can't think of anything that has provided more solace and wonder in my life than this simple exchange with mother earth.

When the Covid-19 pandemic locked down the world a few years ago, I was and am still emphatically grateful for the fact that one could still be outdoors. I'm not sure how I would've survived without this.

John and I would walk 2-3 times a day and witness the blossoms of that Spring that so many people may have missed. I will never forget how fragrant and abundant those blossoms were. We marveled at how empty all the spaces we inhabited were. We felt blessed to experience that Springtime, and the simplicity of it seemed profound in those early Covid days. Every walk was filled with sights and sounds and fragrances that became the centerpiece for our long and quiet days.

Those days were filled with worry too, about everything we could lose. It is sad to think of everyone who lost everything that Spring and the months that followed.

It makes a person take stock of what matters most, and I always came to the same conclusion that no matter where you rest your head at night, health, freedom, warmth, security, fellowship, and love; these are the simplest of needs, and yet they are elusive to many. Time marched on as it does, and the disaster of Covid was behind us, only to find a new disaster to lament. The terrible news that has existed across continents since the beginning of time has found its way into our everyday lives as often as we choose to look into a screen or read the paper.

Many things have changed, and yet so many things remain the same. I hope that we can make meaningful progress as we protect the future of the planet, so that our grandchildren will enjoy nature's simplest of pleasures. The freedom to breathe and to explore out in nature and to experience an appreciation and understanding of the natural world along the way. I believe happiness is amplified through nature and we must protect this intimate partner in our lives.

Nature has always been my best friend for she is the best listener, and the feedback is always filled with outstanding information. When we listen for sounds… she whispers back to us and her whispers are truth. They are energizing, nurturing, healing, they are whispers of whatever it is we might need.

The beauty that surrounds us is meant to reveal pathways for humanity, for peace, harmony, and simplicity. We need the abundance of nature not only to survive, but to share with others and to experience empathy and a healthy humanity. Earth provides us with everything; it feeds our souls and our bodies, and it informs us and guides us through the chapters of our lives.

My life has been filled with many incredibly happy days, and I want this for all children. May their little lives be filled to the brim with promise, smiles, full bellies, and freedom.

We can surely think of a special day when you can't stop smiling. Where the sun feels like a giant ray of supreme love shining right down on you. It finds you right where you are standing.

Where the earth smells pristine in the same way a new

baby smells. Where you feel like you are walking on this golden sunshine, and everything is possible.

Of course, special occasions fall into this category. I remember my son's and my daughter's wedding days - the way they looked, the way they smiled with such intense happiness at their new life partners. Those smiles are in my soul and will be carried with me into the ethers. Our lives are made of moments. Some make you smile; some make you cry and all make you human.

Time continues to march forward, and yet for good reason, it will never erase the indelible memories. As a child, I watched my Tata Zarifeh grow old and pass, and then some of my aunts and uncles too. And then the loss of my sweet father hit me with the deepest sorrow. After some time, I learned how to share a permanent space with him, and this is something that I hope my children will be able to do when I pass on. It is wonderful to still 'see' my father in a way that nourishes my soul.

Watching my father age and become ill, and now my mother slowly fading into another world, is painful, yet it is the simple truth for all of us. My children will have that experience when my time here is done, and then they are next in line and then their own children after that. This could be sad to think about, but I choose to see it as one of the beautiful chapters of a life well-lived.

I believe that our happiness starts from within, radiates outwards and collects information from experiences and memories, and draws them back to you, and each of us gets to determine what we hold on to from all that we have gathered along the way.

In case you haven't noticed by now, my mind wanders. It meanders over, under, and beyond. It brings me great joy with its simple desire to find beauty and kindness.

I don't know what comes next.

I don't need to know.

I know that I am so truly fortunate and that my blessings are many.

I live my life; I send my prayers into the universe, and I move along the river of life. When I get hung up in the reeds or fallen branches, it is with the deepest intention that I push off the banks of the river until I free myself once again. I keep heading down that river through sunny skies, and even when they are sometimes turbulent and gray, it is always with the deepest optimism, love, and determination to cherish and honor my family that propels me forward.

Me and Sunflowers Walnut Creek 2020

Mom and I in the vineyard with a bunch of warak dawali and some Ceja Wine.

Appreciation

Thank you for being here with me. These are my stories, and I have shared them openly. It's like a nakedness to tell your stories. But not to tell them is their burial. I have found great comfort in this storytelling because it unearths all that came before and leaves it here to breathe and exist long after I am gone.

Thank you to my beautiful family for helping me on this journey, and to my ancestors for always cheering me on and reminding me of my beautiful roots.

May the roots of Palestine thrive eternally in Palestine and across the many continents where they have been planted.

About the Author

Patricia J. Mousa, a first-generation Palestinian American, was born in the Detroit area. She now resides in Northern California, where she continues to draw inspiration from her rich cultural heritage. With a distinguished career working with independent grocers in the specialty foods industry, Patricia has a keen appreciation for unique flavors and culinary traditions. She is the proud mother of two children and a grandmother (Tayta) to four, weaving her family's experiences and traditions into her writing. Her life experiences and heritage inspire her writing, offering readers a unique and heartfelt perspective.

ABOOKS

ALIVE Book Publishing and ALIVE Publishing Group
are imprints of Advanced Publishing LLC,
3200 A Danville Blvd., Suite 204, Alamo, California 94507

Telephone: 925.837.7303 Fax: 925.837.6951
www.alivebookpublishing.com

www.ingramcontent.com/pod-product-compliance
Lightning Source LLC
LaVergne TN
LVHW041114080826
845145LV00007B/1809

* 9 7 8 1 6 3 1 3 2 2 6 7 9 *